The Essential Guide

RESEARCH WRITING
ACROSS THE DISCIPLINES

Third Edition

James D. Lester, Sr.
Austin Peay State University

James D. Lester, Jr.
Clayton College and State University

PEARSON
Longman

New York San Francisco Boston
London Toronto Sydney Tokyo Singapore Madrid
Mexico City Munich Paris Cape Town Hong Kong Montreal

Senior Vice President and Publisher: Joseph Opiela
Marketing Manager: Deborah Murphy
Senior Supplements Editor: Donna Campion
Production Manager: Douglas Bell
Project Coordination, Text Design, and Electronic Page Makeup: Electronic
    Publishing Services Inc., NYC
Cover Designer/Manager: Nancy Danahy
Senior Manufacturing Buyer: Dennis J. Para
Printer and Binder: Webcrafters, Inc.
Cover Printer: The Lehigh Press, Inc.

For permission to use copyrighted material, grateful acknowledgment is
made to the copyright holders on p. 203, which is hereby made part of
this copyright page.

Library of Congress Cataloging-in-Publication Data

Lester, James D.
    The essential guide : research writing across the disciplines / James D.
      Lester, Sr., James D. Lester, Jr.– 3rd ed.
      p. cm.
      Includes bibliographical references and indexes.
      ISBN 0-321-27639-6
    1. Report writing–Handbooks, manuals, etc. 2. Research–Handbooks,
    manuals, etc. I. Lester, James D. II. Title.
    LB2369.L47 2005
    808'.02–dc22   2004005538

Please visit us at http://www.ablongman.com

ISBN 0-321-27639-6

    4 5 6 7 8 9 10—WC—07 06

Contents

Preface

This third edition of *The Essential Guide: Research Writing across the Disciplines* has several new features to serve students and instructors in first-year composition courses as well as beginning researchers in the social and physical sciences. In brief, it serves by providing:

- Well-focused information on electronic research
- Help with electronic presentations
- A new focus on critical reading with an emphasis on academic integrity
- Thorough discussions on composing from sources
- Writing methods in the various disciplines
- Current information from the most recent style guides
- New student papers
- An ancillary package

Electronic Research

The text explores the new aspects of library research. It spotlights the academic databases that can be accessed only through the library's electronic system. It encourages controlled Internet searches but sets guidelines for acceptable academic sites. In field research, it helps students conduct interviews, questionnaires, and correspondence by e-mail and Web conferencing. The text provides students with a comprehensive list, by discipline, of important reference tools.

Electronic Presentations

The Essential Guide has a complete chapter for students who wish to present their research project electronically. The chapter explains the methods for developing the research paper with slide presentations, Web pages, Web sites, and digital graphics. It also explains the methods for delivering the paper by e-mail, Zip drive, CD-ROM, and Web site.

An Emphasis on Academic Integrity

Electronic retrieval has made plagiarism a pesky problem, so a new chapter, short but to the point, on what constitutes plagiarism has been added. The same passage is reproduced repeatedly to demonstrate the differences between writing that cites sources properly and writing that fails in blatant and subtle ways the test of plagiarism.

Focus on Critical Reading

Chapters 6 and 7 now give invaluable tips to students on such matters as identifying the best sources, evaluating them for relevance, authority, and accuracy, and—just as important—creating notes that summarize, quote, and paraphrase effectively and to a point. This section shows students how to use their notes to build an annotated bibliography and a review of the literature on a narrowed topic.

Composing with Sources

The Essential Guide helps students find good sources, create effective notes in a variety of fashions, and then—most important of all—blend those sources into an effective piece of writing, expressed in the student's voice yet supported by the sources. Thus, Chapters 8 and 9 on blending sources for an academic style are vital if students hope to honor the conventions of research style.

Writing in the Disciplines

The default style for instruction in this text is the MLA style for students and instructors in literature and composition. However, the book also explores research style through the lenses of disciplines in the social sciences, natural sciences, applied sciences, and humanities.

Science students examine and test a hypothesis, while literature students build on a thesis statement. Science students do more field research than students in philosophy or history. In addition, science students do different things with their testing and their comments on the results. Thus, several aspects of academic writing are examined and explained in this book—the footnote system, the name and year system, and the number system.

Keeping Current to the Latest Standards

This new edition of *The Essential Guide: Research Writing across the Disciplines* has been updated to conform to these basic style guides:

Chicago Manual of Style, 15th edition, 2003

MLA Handbook for Writers of Research Papers, 6th edition, 2003

Publication Manual of the American Psychological Association, 5th edition, 2002

Scientific Style and Format: The CSE Manual for Authors, Editors, and Publishers, 7th edition, 2004

New Student Papers

To demonstrate MLA style, the text includes three papers:
"Annotated Bibliography" by Norman Levenson
"Gender Communication: A Review of the Literature" by Kaci Holz
"Listening to *Hamlet:* The Soliloquies" by Melinda Mosier

To demonstrate APA style, the text features:
"Arranged Marriages: The Revival Is Online" by Valerie Nesbitt-Hall

To show the CMS footnote style, the text displays:
"Prehistorical Wars: We've Always Hated Each Other" by Jamie Johnston

To demonstrate the CSE number style, the text presents:
"Diabetes Management: A Delicate Balance" by Sarah Bemis

The Ancillary Package

The publication package includes these features:

- *E-mail access to the authors.* We are available to instructors and students to answer questions on style and format.
- *Instructor's Manual.* This handy guide contains chapter-by-chapter classroom exercises, research assignments, quizzes, and duplication masters; it is available to instructors on request.

Acknowledgments

We wish to thank those who have been instrumental in the development of *The Essential Guide: Research Writing across the Disciplines,* 3rd edition: Darin Cozzens, Surry Community College; David Rivers, Loyola College, Maryland; Christopher Buck, Michigan State University; and Dr. Gayle Bolt Price, Gardner-Webb University.

We thank student authors Norman Berkowitz, Valerie Nesbitt-Hall, Jamie Johnston, Norman Levenson, Kaci Holz, and Sarah Bemis. Our love goes to our family members: Martha, Mark, Debbie, Caleb, and Sarah.

James D. Lester, Sr.
jamesdlester@aol.com
Clarksville, TN

James D. Lester, Jr.
jameslester@mail.clayton.edu
Morrow, GA

1

Finding a Scholarly Topic

You will seldom go in search of a topic so much as you will focus a preexisting general subject, one given to you by the instructor or one that you have wanted to explore but had no reason for doing so. As you move from class to class, keep your focus on the issues of each course. A health class might suggest this topic to somebody who smokes and who has a family to worry about: "Secondhand Smoke: Is It a Firsthand Danger?" A literature instructor might require you to explore Nathaniel Hawthorne's fiction, which is nineteenth-century material, but you can make it contemporary: "Hester Prynne in the Twenty-First Century: Who Wears the Scarlet Letter Today?" Notice how two students focused their topics.

- Valerie Nesbitt-Hall saw a cartoon about a young woman saying to a man, "Sorry—I only have relationships over the Internet. I'm cybersexual." Although she laughed, Valerie knew she had discovered a good topic in "online romance." Upon investigation, she found her scholarly focus: Matching services and chat rooms are like the arranged marriages from years gone by. You can read her paper on pages 158–66: "Arranged Marriages: The Revival Is Online."
- Jamie Johnston, while watching reports on the Iraqi War, noticed the bitterness of the fighting and the cruelty practiced on both sides of the conflict. Shocking to him was the abuse of prisoners by American forces. He raised a crucial question that pointed him toward his research: How can civilized people in this day and age act with such violence against fellow human beings? He began by investigating prehistoric warfare. Ultimately, his title expressed his thesis: "Prehistoric Wars: We've Always Hated Each Other." You can read Jamie's paper on pages 175–180.

These topics meet the expectations of composition instructors as well as those of instructors in health, sociology, political science, education, and many other disciplines. Consider the following list of possible topics:

EDUCATION:	The Visually Impaired: Options for Classroom Participation
POLITICAL SCIENCE:	The Impact of the Presidential Electoral College
HEALTH:	The Effects of Chemicals on Athletic Performance
SOCIOLOGY:	Parents Who Lie to Their Children: Psychological Consequences

1a   Generating Ideas and Focusing the Subject

You can generate ideas for research and focus on the issues with a number of techniques:

- Relate your personal ideas to a scholarly problem.
- Talk with others.
- Examine electronic sources.
- Read textbooks and reference books.

Relating Your Personal Ideas to a Scholarly Problem

Draw on yourself for ideas, keep a research journal, ask yourself questions, and get comfortable with new terminology.

Personal Ideas

Draw on yourself for inspiration and direction. Contemplate the issues and generate ideas worthy of investigation. At a quiet time, begin writing, questioning, and pushing on the buttons of your mind for your feelings and attitudes. The research paper should reflect your thinking in response to the sources. It should not merely report what others have said. If possible, combine a personal interest with one aspect of your academic studies:

ACADEMIC SUBJECT:	Health, especially sports medicine
PERSONAL INTEREST:	Skiing
POSSIBLE TOPICS:	Protecting the Knees
	Therapy for Strained Muscles
	Skin Treatments

You might also consider social issues that affect you and your family:

ACADEMIC SUBJECT:	Education

PERSONAL INTEREST:	The behavior of my child in school
POSSIBLE TOPICS:	Calming Children Who Are Hyperactive
	Should Schoolchildren Take Medicine to
	Calm Their Hyperactivity?

Your cultural background can prompt you toward detailed research into your roots, your culture, and the mythology and history of your ethnic background:

ACADEMIC SUBJECT:	History
ETHNIC BACKGROUND:	Native Americans
PERSONAL INTEREST:	History of the Apache tribes
POSSIBLE TOPIC:	The Indian Wars from the Native
	American's Point of View

A Research Journal

Unlike a diary of personal thoughts about your daily activities or a journal of creative ideas, such as poems, stories, and scenarios, the research journal enables you to list issues, raise questions, create notes, and develop pieces of free writing. In fact, you should build the journal primarily with **free writing** as well as **keywords and phrases** that come to mind. These establish primary categories for your research. One student listed several terms and phrases about the use of midwives in the rural Southeastern mountains:

natural childbirth	disinfectants	recovery time
prenatal care	medicines	delivery
hardships	complications	sterilization
delivery problems	deaths	cost

In her research journal, she began writing notes on these topics, like this:

The cost of delivery by a midwife in the mother's home differs so greatly from the cost of a doctor and a hospital that we can only appreciate the plight of those using this procedure.

The research journal is also a place for preliminary outlining to find the major and minor issues, as shown here:

Midwives in the Rural Southeast Mountains

Preparation:	Delivery:	Recovery:	Cost:
prenatal care	natural childbirth	after delivery	one fee
sterilization	medicines	recovery time	
disinfectants	delivery techniques	deaths	

Questions

Asking questions in your research journal can focus your attention on primary issues, and your subsequent notes in answer to the questions can launch your investigation. For example, having read Henry Thoreau's essay "Civil Disobedience," one writer posed these questions:

What is civil disobedience?
Is dissent legal? Is it moral? Is it patriotic?
Is dissent a liberal activity? Conservative?
Should the government encourage or stifle dissent?
Is passive resistance effective?

Answering the questions can lead the writer to a central issue or argument, such as "Civil Disobedience: Shaping Our Nation."

Academic disciplines across the curriculum invite questions that might provoke a variety of answers and give focus to the subject, as with "sports gambling."

ECONOMICS:	Does sports gambling benefit a college's athletic budget? Does it benefit the national economy?
PSYCHOLOGY:	What is the effect of gambling on the mental attitude of the college athlete who knows that huge sums hang in the balance on his/her performance?
HISTORY:	Does gambling on sporting events have an identifiable tradition?
SOCIOLOGY:	What compulsion in human nature prompts people to gamble on athletic prowess?
POLITICAL SCIENCE:	What laws exist in this state for the control of illegal sports gambling? Are they enforced?

Terminology

Each discipline has its own terminology. For example, in researching a paper on retail marketing you might learn to refer to "the demographics" of a "target audience." In psychological research, you might learn to use the phrases "control group" and "experimental group." One student found essential words for her paper on diabetes:

diabetes	diabetes mellitus	glucose
insulin	metabolize	hyperglycemia
pancreas	ketoacidosis	ketones

She learned the meaning of each term and applied it properly in her paper, giving her work a scholarly edge.

Talking with Others to Find and Refine the Topic

Sometime early in your project, go outside yourself to get feedback on your possible topic and its issues. You can accomplish this task with personal interviews, participation in e-mail discussion groups, and, on a limited basis, in Internet chat forums.

Personal Interview

A personal interview, either face to face, by telephone, or by e-mail, allows you to consult with experts and people in your community for ideas and reactions to your subject. Explore a subject for key ideas while having coffee or a soda with a colleague, relative, or work associate. For example, Valerie Nesbitt-Hall researched online matchmaking. She knew of one married couple who had met while chatting on the Internet. She requested an interview by e-mail, secured it, and made that interview a vital part of her paper. You can see Valerie's paper on pages 158–66.

> **HINT:** Casual conversations that contribute to your understanding of the subject need not be documented. However, a formal interview or an in-depth discussion with an expert demands credit in your text and a citation in the Works Cited page at the end of your paper.

Local E-mail Discussion Group

Many instructors establish e-mail discussion groups for their courses to meet the demands of special interest groups. These discussion boards are popular with online courses, especially those using the Blackboard software for course management. These are private sites reserved for class members and the instructors, so they focus on the specific interests of the group. Thus, you can get input from your peers as well as your instructor, and you can make pertinent queries about your subject matter.

Internet Discussion Group

During an online chat conversation, you might find a few ideas on your topic; however, *heed this warning:* participants use fictitious names, provide unreliable sources, are highly opinionated in most instances, and therefore *they cannot be quoted in your paper.* The best you might gain is marginal insight into the ideas of people who are often eccentric and who hide behind their anonymity.

Using Electronic Sources

The library is your best source for electronic articles. Start with the library's academic databases and its electronic book catalog. After that, search the World Wide Web. You might also examine CDs and videotapes.

Library Databases

Go to the reliable databases available through your library, such as InfoTrac, PsychINFO, UMI ProQuest, Electric Library, and EBSCO-host. You can reach these from remote locations at home or the dorm room by connecting to your library with your personal identification number. The library has monitored Internet sites filtered by editorial boards and peer review. Many articles on these databases appeared first in print. In many cases, you can read an abstract of the article before reading the full text. You can also print the article without going into the stacks. However, libraries vary in their access to electronic databases, so be sure to consult with the reference librarians.

Electronic Book Catalogs

Use your library's computerized index to find books, film, DVD holdings, and similar items. Entering a keyword, such as "George W. Bush," yields a listing of relevant books—in this case, books by and about the president. The book catalog does not index the titles to articles in magazines and journals, but it can tell you which periodicals are housed in the library and whether they are in a printed volume, on microforms, or in an electronic database (see immediately above). Instructors want you to consult books during your research, so follow these steps:

1. Enter a keyword, such as "nutrition," that will generate a reasonably sized list.
2. Examine the entries in detail, starting with the most recent, to find books related to your topic.
3. In the stacks, find and examine each book for relevance. *Tip*: While in the stacks examine nearby books, which may well treat the same subject.

World Wide Web

Articles on the Internet offer ideas about how other people approach the subject, and these ideas can help you refine your topic. Use the subject directory on a browser, such as Google, to probe from a general topic to specific articles (Health > Diseases > Blood disorders > Anemia). Use a keyword search when you already have a specific topic. Thus, entering the keyword "anemia" will send you immediately to various Web articles. See Chapter 3, pages 32–45, for more about searching the Internet.

CD-ROM, DVD, VHS

Encarta, Electronic Classical Library, Compton's Interactive Encyclopedia, and other reference diskettes are available. Browsing at one of these sources will give you a good feel for the depth and strength of the subject and suggest a list of narrowed topics. Check with a librarian, a department office, and your instructor for disks and videos in a specialty area, such as mythology, poetry, or American history. These media forms can sometimes be found in local bookstores or purchased over the Internet.

Using Textbooks and Reference Books

Dipping into your own textbooks can reward you with topic ideas, and a trip to the library to examine books and indexes in the reference room can also be beneficial.

Library Books and Textbooks

With your working topic in hand, do some exploratory reading. Carefully examine the **titles** of books, noting key terminology. Search a book's **table of contents** for topics. A history book on the American Civil War might display these headings:

The Clash of Amateur Armies
Real Warfare Begins
The Navies
Confederate High-Water Mark

If any heading looks interesting to you, go to the book's **index** for additional headings, such as this sample:

Jefferson Davis, President of the Confederate States
    evacuates Richmond, 574, 576
    foreign relations, 250, 251
    imprisonment of, 567
    inauguration, 52–53
    peace proposals, 564–65

Perhaps the topic on peace proposals will spur your interest in all peace proposals—that is, how nations end wars and send their troops home safely.

Reference Books

If you do not have access to an electronic database, the printed indexes, such as the *Readers' Guide to Periodical Literature, Bibliographic Index,* and *Humanities Index,* categorize and subdivide topics by alphabetical order. Searching under a keyword or phrase usually leads to a list of critical articles on the subject, and studying the titles might suggest a narrowed topic. For example, looking under the heading "Single Mothers" might produce several possible topics, such as "Welfare Moms," "Single Motherhood," or "Racial Differentials in Child Support."

> **HINT:** Topic selection goes beyond choosing a general category (e.g., "single mothers"). It includes finding a research-provoking issue or question, such as "The foster parent program seems to have replaced the orphanage system. Has it been effective?" That is, you need to take a stand, adopt a belief, or begin asking questions. For more information, see section 1c, "Drafting a Research Proposal."

1b Writing a Thesis, Enthymeme, or Hypothesis

Usually, one central statement controls an essay's direction and content, so as early as possible, begin thinking in terms of a controlling idea. Each type shown below has a separate mission:

- A **thesis sentence** advances a conclusion the writer will defend: *Contrary to what some philosophers have advanced, human beings have always participated in wars.*
- An **enthymeme** uses a *because* clause to make a claim the writer will defend: *There has never been a "noble savage," as such, because even prehistoric human beings fought frequent wars for numerous reasons.*
- A **hypothesis** is a theory that must be tested in the laboratory, in the literature, and/or by field research to prove its validity: *Human beings are motivated by biological instincts toward the physical overthrow of perceived enemies.*

Each type is discussed next.

Thesis Statement

A thesis sentence expands your topic into a scholarly proposal, one that you will try to prove and defend in your paper. It does not state the obvious, such as "Langston Hughes was a great poet from Harlem." That sentence cannot provoke an academic discussion because readers know that any published poet has talent. The writer must isolate one issue by finding a critical focus, such as this one:

> Langston Hughes used a controversial vernacular language that paved the way for later artists, even today's rap musicians.

This sentence advances an idea that the writer can develop fully and defend with evidence. The writer has made a connection between the subject, Langston Hughes, and the focusing agent, vernacular language. A general thesis might state:

> Certain nutritional foods can prevent disease.

But note how your interest in an academic area can color the thesis:

HEALTH: Nutritional foods may be a promising addition to the diet of people wishing to avoid certain diseases.

ECONOMICS: Nutritional foods can become an economic weapon in the battle against rising health care costs.

HISTORY: Other civilizations, including primitive tribes, have known about food's nutritional values for centuries. We can learn from their knowledge.

A thesis sets in motion the writer's examination of specific ideas the study will explore and defend. Thus, when confronted by a general topic, such as "television," adjust it to an academic interest, as with "Video replays have improved football officiating but slowed the game" or "Video technology has enhanced arthroscopic surgery."

Your thesis is not your conclusion or your answer to a problem. Rather, it anticipates your conclusion by setting in motion the examination of facts and pointing the reader toward the special idea of your paper, which you save for the conclusion.

Enthymeme

Some of your instructors might want the research paper to develop an argument as expressed in an enthymeme, which consists of two parts: a claim supported with a *because* clause. However, you need to understand that the enthymeme has a structure that depends on one or more unstated assumptions.

> Hyperactive children need medication because ADHD is a medical disorder, not a behavioral problem.

The claim that hyperactive children need medication is supported by the stated reason that the condition is a medical problem, not one of behavior. This writer must address the unstated assumption that medication alone will solve the problem.

> Participating in one of the martial arts, such as Tae Kwan Do, is good for children because it promotes self-discipline.

The claim that one organized sporting activity is good for children rests on the value of self-discipline. Unstated is the assumption that one sport, the martial arts, is good for children in other areas of development, such as physical conditioning. The writer might also address other issues, such as aggression or a combat mentality.

Hypothesis

A hypothesis is a theory that must be tested to prove its validity and an assumption advanced for the purpose of argument or investigation. Here's an example:

> Discrimination against girls and young women in the classroom, known as <u>shortchanging</u>, harms the chances of women to develop fully academically.

This statement could lead to a theoretical study if the student cites literature on the ways in which teachers shortchange students. A professional educator, on the other hand, would probably conduct extensive research in many classroom settings to defend the hypothesis with scientific observation.

Sometimes the hypothesis is *conditional:*

> Our campus has a higher crime rate than other state colleges.

This assertion on a conditional state of being could be tested by statistical comparison. At other times the hypothesis is *relational:*

> Class size affects the number of written assignments given by writing instructors.

This type of hypothesis claims that as one variable changes, so does another, or that something is more or less than another. It could be tested by examining and correlating class size and assignments.

At other times, the researcher produces a *causal hypothesis:*

> A child's choice of a toy is determined by television commercials.

Narrowing a General Subject into a Working Topic

Unlike a general subject, a focused topic should:

- Examine one significant issue, not a broad subject.
- Argue from a thesis sentence, enthymeme, or hypothesis.
- Address a knowledgeable reader and carry that reader to another plateau of knowledge.
- Have a serious purpose, one that demands analysis of the issues, argues from a position, and explains complex details.
- Meet the expectations of the instructor and conform to the course requirements.

This causal hypothesis assumes the mutual occurrence of two factors and asserts that one factor is responsible for the other. The student who is a parent could conduct research to prove or disprove the supposition.

Thus, your paper, motivated by a hypothesis, might be a theoretical examination of the literature or field study on such topics as the diet of migrating geese, the yield of one species of hybrid corn, or the behavior of children as they watch violence on television. See also pages 46–54 for more information on field research.

1c   Drafting a Research Proposal

A research proposal helps clarify and focus a research project. It comes in two forms: (1) a short paragraph that identifies the project for approval of your instructor, or (2) several pages that give background information, your rationale for conducting the study, a review of the literature, your methods, and the thesis, enthymeme, or hypothesis you plan to defend.

Writing a Short Research Proposal

A short proposal identifies five essential ingredients of your project:

1. The specific topic.
2. The purpose of the paper (explain, analyze, argue).
3. The intended audience (general or specialized).

4. Your position as the writer (informer, interpreter, evaluator, reviewer).
5. The preliminary thesis sentence or opening hypothesis.

One writer developed this brief proposal:

> The world is running out of fresh water while we sip our Evian. However, the bottled water craze signals something— we don't trust our fresh tap water. We have an emerging crisis on our hands, and some authorities forecast world wars over water rights. The issue of water touches almost every facet of our lives, from religious rituals and food supply to disease and political instability. We might frame this hypothesis: Water will soon replace oil as the economic resource most treasured by nations of the world. However, that assertion would prove difficult to defend and may not be true at all. Rather, we need to look elsewhere, at human behavior, and at human responsibility for preserving the environment for our children. Accordingly, this paper will examine (1) the issues with regard to supply and demand, (2) the political power struggles that may emerge, and (3) the ethical implications for those who control the world's scattered supply of fresh water.

Writing a Detailed Research Proposal

A long proposal presents specific details concerning the project. It has more depth and length than the short proposal shown above. The long proposal should include some or all of the following elements:

1. *Cover page* with the title of the project, your name, and the person or agency to whom you are submitting the proposal (see pages 109–10 for details on writing titles and pages 140–41 for the form of a title page).
2. An *abstract* that summarizes your project in 50 to 100 words (see page 159 for an example).
3. A *purpose statement* with your *rationale* for the project (see the short proposal above for an example). Use *explanation* to review and itemize factual data. One writer explained how diabetes can be managed (see Sarah Bemis's essay on pages 184–89). Use *analysis* to classify parts of the subject and to investigate each one in depth (see Melinda Mosier's paper on Shakespeare's soliloquies).

Use *persuasion* to question general attitudes about a problem and then to affirm new theories, advance a solution, recommend a course of action, or—in the least—invite the reader into an intellectual dialog (see Jamie Johnston's paper on prehistoric wars, pages 175–80).

4. A *statement of qualification* that explains your experience and perhaps the special qualities you bring to the project (i.e., you are the parent of a child with ADHD). If you have no experience with the subject, you can omit the statement of qualification.

5. A *review of the literature* that surveys the articles and books you have examined in your preliminary work (see pages 95–102 for an explanation and an example of a review of literature).

6. A presentation of your *research methods,* which is a description of the design of the *materials* you will need, your *timetable* for completing the project, and, when applicable, your *budget.* These elements are often a part of a scientific study, so see Chapters 10 and 11 for work in the social, physical, and biological sciences.

2

Library Research

With a refined topic in hand, you can begin research in three different places—the library, the Internet, and the field. The next three chapters will explore these options.

2a Finding Sources with Your Library Access

You can begin your research from your apartment, your dorm room, a computer lab, or the library itself. All you need is online access to the library with your student identification. Your initial strategy normally includes three stages: the initial search to gauge the academic atmosphere for your subject, fine-tuning your focus for in-depth searching, and building your own electronic journal with a working bibliography, printouts, and downloaded items. In addition, it pays for you to stroll through your library to identify its sections and make mental notes of the types of information available there.

Begin your search at the library's electronic book catalog and electronic databases because they will:

- Show the availability of source materials with diverse opinions.
- Provide a beginning set of reference citations, abstracts, full-text articles, and books, some of which can be printed or downloaded.
- Help restrict the subject and narrow your focus.
- Give an overview of the subject by showing how others have discussed it.

HINT: Today's college library not only houses academic books and periodicals but also connects you via the Internet to thousands of academic resources you cannot reach any other way. Whether you visit the library in person or by computer link, you are assured of getting sources that have been reviewed carefully and judged worthy of your time and interest. This differs from a general Internet browser, which cannot access the scholarly material at the academic sites. A general browser, such as Google or Lycos, might send you anywhere. The library's databases will send you to reputable sources.

2b   Using the Library's Electronic Book Catalog

Your library's computerized catalog probably has a name such as LIBNET, FELIX, ACORN, or UTSEARCH. It serves as your primary source for several items.

Books

The catalog lists every book in the library by subject, author, and title along with the call number, location in the stacks, and availability, as shown in this example:

Research: Successful Approaches Elaine R. Monsen, ed.
Subjects: Nutrition research / Dietetics research
Location: General Book Collection, Level 3
Call number: TX367.R46 2003
Status: Available

In many cases, clicking on the title gives you an abstract of the book. Sometimes the library's catalog also provides access to electronic books on the World Wide Web, as shown in this example, which provides a hyperlink:

Nutrition in Early Life [electronic resource]
Edited by Jane B. Morgan and John W. T. Dickerson
Internet access: http://www.netLibrary.com/urlapi.asp
    ?action=summary&v=1&bookid=79551

Journals

The catalog includes references to journals in bound volumes physically housed at the library or electronically on the Internet, with links for accessing them.

Journal of Nutrition Education and Behavior
Availability: Periodicals Collection, Level 1
This journal is available at the library.

The American Journal of Clinical Nutrition [electronic resource]
Internet access: Full text available from Highwire Press (Free
    Journals)
http://highwire.standford.edu/lists/freeart.dtl

This journal, not housed in the library, is accessed only by clicking on the hyperlink. We discuss this feature in the next section, 2c

Internet Sites

The catalog includes hyperlinks to Web sites the librarians have
identified as excellent academic sources. See, for example, the catalog entry for this government document:

Food and Nutrition [electronic resource]
Washington, DC: Food and Nutrition Service, U.S. Dept. of Agri-
    culture
Internet access: Full text available from Health and Wellness
    Resource http://morris.lib.apsu.edu/rpa/
    webauth.exe?rs = wellness

Reference Books

The electronic catalog also lists reference books. It indexes by
call number those housed in the library. Those available online have
hypertext links.

Essay and General Literature Index
H. W. Wilson Company
Location: Reference Stacks, Level 2
Status: Available
Call number: A13 .E752

Social Sciences [electronic resource]
Internet access: Full text available from Columbia International
    Affairs Online http://www.ciaonet.org/

Archives

Archival research takes you into past literature so you can trace
developing issues and ideas on a subject.

Archives of Dermatology [electronic resource]
Internet access: Full text available from InfoTrac http://
    morris.lib.apsu.edu/rpa/webauth.exe?rs=eai

Bibliographies

Bibliographies list the works by a writer or the works about a subject. They give you access to the titles of articles and books on your
topic, usually up to a certain date, as shown in this next resource.

Bibliography of Tobacco-Related Literature on Hispanic/Latinos,
    1990–2001 [electronic resource]

National Cancer Institute, U.S. Dept of Health and Human
Services
Internet access: http://purl.access.gpo.gov/GPO/LPS19290

HINT: Many college libraries as well as public libraries are now
part of library networks. A network expands the holdings of
every member library because each library loans books to
another. Therefore, if a book you need is unavailable in your
library, ask a librarian about an interlibrary loan. Understand,
however, that you may have to wait several days for its delivery.
Periodical articles usually arrive quickly by fax or e-mail transfer.

2c Searching the Library's Electronic Databases

At the computer, search the library's network of electronic databases. You will find a list of these search engines at a link on the
library's home page, usually near the electronic book catalog. Each
one has a singular mission: to take you directly to articles on your subject, with abstracts in most cases and full text in many others. Thus,
you can print or download numerous documents, all relevant to your
subject. For example, InfoTrac is a popular database because it covers many subjects. This list gives a few of the sources found by searching on the keyword *coffee*.

Acrylamide found in coffee. (ingredients). (Brief Article)
  Food Engineering & Ingredients Dec 2002 v27 i6 p35(1)
  (88 words)
Text

The complexity of coffee: One of life's simple pleasure is really
  quite complex (growth, harvesting, processing, and brewing)
  Ernesto Illy
Scientific American June 2002 v286 i6 p86(6) (2993 words)
Text

Muddy waters: The lore, the lure, the lowdown on America's
  favorite addiction (coffee, coffee madness)
(Cover story) Mark Schapiro
Utne Reader Nov–Dec 1994 n66 p58(8)
Abstract

Clicking on an underlined hyperlink accesses the article for your
use. As shown above, the third source provides an abstract only, but the

first two citations provide the full text of the article, which you ca
print or download to your files. Remember to save them as text file

General Databases

In addition to InfoTrac, there are many other general database
to serve your initial investigation. These databases are sometimes ger
eral in order to index many articles on a wide variety of topics. Star
with one of these if you have a general keyword for your research bu
not a specific and focused topic.

BOOKS IN PRINT:	This database lists all books cur-rently in print and available from publishers.
CQ RESEARCHER:	This collection provides in-depth reports on topics of current interest.
ENCYCLOPEDIA BRITANNICA:	This reference covers all subjects with brief, well-organized articles
FIRSTSEARCH:	This database covers a wide vari ety of topics and directs you to both articles and books.
GPO:	This site for the U.S. Govern-ment Printing Office gives you access to all government publica tions on all subjects.
INFORME!:	This database offers an index to articles in Spanish-language magazines.
INGENTA:	This site provides general informa tion on a vast variety of topics. However, it is a commercial site, and you must pay for articles you download or order by fax.
NETLIBRARY:	This database carries you to books on all subjects, including e-books. To access a book online, you need both a user-name and a password; these are available from a librarian.
ONLINE BOOKS PAGE:	Maintained by the University of Pennsylvania, this site gives you access to books on all subjects, with options for printing and downloading.

OXFORD REFERENCE ONLINE: This database offers you the full text of 135 reference books published by Oxford University Press. The sources cover all general subjects. See your librarian to secure the username and password necessary for entry into the database.

By investigating two or three of the databases listed above, you should gain a quick start on your initial investigation into a subject. The sources you download or print will help focus your topic and help you frame your thesis sentence.

Databases by Discipline

Your library also houses subject-specific databases. Thus, you can examine a specialized database for articles on health issues or, if you prefer, history, and many others. Listed next, by subject area, are a few databases to help launch your investigation. Note: These sources are available only through libraries, and in some cases they require an additional username and password that you must request from your librarian.

Literature

CONTEMPORARY LITERARY CRITICISM: A database that indexes critical articles about contemporary authors. It is thus a good source if you are examining the work of a twenty–first-century writer.

LION: This database provides full-text poems, drama, and fiction. It includes biographies, literary criticism, guides to analysis of literary works, and even video readings by writers.

LITFINDER: This source is a search engine for finding poems, stories, plays, and essays.

MLA BIBLIOGRAPHY: This is a major database for all significant articles of criticism on literature, linguistics, and folklore.

History

AMERICA: HISTORY AND LIFE: This is a first-rate database covering all the important articles in this area.

WORLD HISTORY

FULLTEXT: A database to full-text articles about all phases of world history.

VIVA: This database focuses on history with an emphasis on women's studies.

Education, Psychology, and Social Issues

ERIC: This giant database takes you quickly to articles and some books with a focus primarily on education but with full coverage of social and communication topics.

PROJECTMUSE: This database provides current issues of about 200 journals in the fields of education, cultural studies, political science, gender studies, literature, and others. It also links you to JSTOR (see the next entry) for past issues of the journals.

JSTOR: The acronym stands for "journal storage" because this database maintains the images of thousands of academic articles in their original form and with original page numbers. It centers on the social sciences but includes articles from other fields, such as literature.

PsycINFO: This database covers a massive index of articles and books in psychology, medicine, education, and social work.

Health, Medicine, Fitness, and Nutrition

CINAHL: The initials stand for Cumulative Index to Nursing and Allied Health Literature, which is a giant database for sources in nursing, public health, and the allied fields of nutrition and fitness.

HEALTH AND WELLNESS: This database indexes a wide array of articles in medicine, nutrition, fitness, and public health.

PUBMED: This source indexes articles on dentistry as well as nursing and medicine.

The Arts

GROVE DICTIONARY OF ART: This source is an online art encyclopedia, not a database. It contains information from the *Dictionary of Art* and features about 45,000 articles on painting, sculpture, architecture, and other visual arts.

GROVE DICTIONARY OF MUSIC: Like the one above, this source is an online encyclopedia with 29,000 articles drawn from the printed versions of the *New Grove Dictionary of Music and Musicians, New Grove Dictionary of Opera,* and *New Grove Dictionary of Jazz.* It covers aspects of music including instrumentation, orchestral performance, and voice.

MUSIC INDEX: This database provides a citation index to 655 journals on a broad range of musical topics, including reviews. However, it is a citation-only database, so no abstracts or full-text are provided. On that subject, however, see the Hint on page 22.

Computers, Business, Technology

GENERAL BUSINESS FILE: This database provides abstracts and some full-text articles on issues in business and industry. It includes company profiles and some Wall Street reports.

SAFARI TECH BOOKS ONLINE: This database focuses on e-commerce and computer science, with information on programming and technology management.

FAITS: The Faulkner Advisory of Information Technology Studies is a database of articles in wireless communications, data networking, security, the Internet, and product comparisons.

The Physical Sciences

AGRICOLA: This database provides an index of articles and book references for agriculture, animal, and plant sciences.

BIOONE: This site provides articles on the biological, ecological, and environmental sciences.

GEOREF: This database carries you to articles in geology and related subjects.

WILEYINTERSCIENCE: This database is loaded with articles on science and biochemistry.

The databases shown above represent just a portion of those available at most college libraries, and more databases are added monthly. Your task is to determine which databases are available at your library and react accordingly. Obviously, small libraries do not have the same online resources as major university libraries. If databases are limited, you may need to consult printed bibliographies and indexes, as discussed in section 2d.

HINT: If the databases to periodicals shown above provide a citation but not the full text, you can probably retrieve the article in one of two ways: (1) using the library's electronic book catalog (see section 2b above) to retrieve the journal itself, or (2) go into the stacks at your library, find the journal, and photocopy the article.

2d Searching the Printed Bibliographies

A bibliography tells you what books and articles are available on a specific subject. If you have a clearly defined topic, skip to page 23, "Searching in the Specialized Bibliographies and Reference Works." If you are still trying to formulate a clear focus, begin with one of these general guides to books to refine your search.

Searching in General Bibliographies

Some works are broad-based references to books on many subjects:

Bibliographic Index: A Cumulative Bibliography of Bibliographies (in print and online)
Where to Find What: A Handbook to Reference Service
Guide to Reference Books

Figure 2.1 shows how *Bibliographic Index* will send you to bibliographic lists inside books. In this case, the bibliography will be found on pages 105–12 of Sarnoff's book.

If it fits your research, you would probably want to write a Works Cited entry for this source, as explained on pages 128–40. The MLA citation would look like this:

Sarnoff, Susan Kiss. <u>Paying for Crime: The Policies and Possibilities of Crime Victim Reimbursement.</u> New York: Praeger, 1996. 105–12.

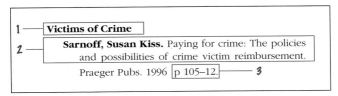

■ FIGURE 2.1

Example from *Bibliographic Index,* 2000, shows (1) subject heading, (2) entry of a book that contains a bibliography on crime, (3) specific pages on which the bibliography is located.

Searching in the Specialized Bibliographies and Reference Works

After you have narrowed your subject, search one or two of the discipline-specific guides and bibliographies listed below under three categories—humanities, social sciences, sciences. In the main, these are well-indexed references that can take you to more specific books. One of them can help you pursue your investigation. Librarians at the reference desk can help you find them, and some are available online.

Humanities

Art	*Bibliographic Guide to Art and Architecture*
	Fine Arts: A Bibliographic Guide
Drama	*American Drama Criticism: Interpretations*
	Cambridge Guide to Theatre
History	*Dictionary of American History*
	Goldentree Bibliographies in History
Literature	*Dictionary of Literary Biography*
	Essay and General Literature Index
Music	*Music Reference and Research Materials*
	Bibliographic Guide to Music
Philosophy	*Oxford Companion to Philosophy*
	Research Guide to Philosophy
Religion	*Reference Works for Theological Research*
	Who's Who in Religion

Social Sciences

Business	*Bibliographic Guide to Business and Economics*
	Business Information Sources
Education	*Education: A Guide to Reference and Information Sources*
	Resources in Education

Social Sciences (continued)

Political | *International Bibliography of Political Science*
Science | *Political Science: A Bibliographical Guide to the Literature*
Psychology | *Annual Reviews of Psychology*
| *Psychology: A Guide to Reference and Information Sources*
| *Bibliographical Guide to Psychology*
Sociology | *References Sources in Social Work*
| *Sociology: A Guide to Reference and Information Sources*
Speech | *Research and Source Guide for Students in Speech Pathology and Audiology*
| *Speech Monographs*
Women's | *American Women Writers: A Critical*
Studies | *Reference Guide*
| *Women's Studies Index*

Sciences

Astronomy | *The Cambridge Atlas of Astronomy*
| *Dictionary of Astronomy*
Biology | *Henderson's Dictionary of Biological Terms*
| *Information Sources in the Life Sciences*
Chemistry | *How to Find Chemical Information: A Guide for Practicing Chemists, Teachers, and Students*
| *Lange's Handbook of Chemistry*
Computer | *ACM Guide to Computing Literature*
Science | *Bibliographic Guide to the History of Computing, Computers, and the Information Processing Industry*
Health | *Black's Medical Dictionary*
| *Cumulated Index Medicus*
Physics | *Information Sources in Physics*
| *Physics Abstracts*

2e   Searching the Printed Indexes

An index furnishes the exact page references of articles in magazines, journals, and newspapers. When you have a well-developed idea of your topic, go to the specialized indexes of your discipline, such as *Music Index* or *Philosopher's Index* (either online at your library's computer or in print at the reference section of your library). Indexes may or may not include abstracts. Those explicitly labeled as indexes to abstracts comprise entries that are abstracts. *Note*: An abstract is a brief description of an article, usually written by its author. An index to abstracts can accelerate your work by allowing you to read summary information about each article before you assume the task of locating and reading the entire work.

Starting with a General Index to Periodicals

A number of indexes are broad based to list articles in journals from many disciplines. These are good places to begin your research because the indexes have multiple entries and, in some cases, the articles are less technical and scholarly than those covered by specialized indexes. For general information on current events, consult *Readers' Guide to Periodical Literature,* which indexes magazines such as *Aging, Foreign Affairs, Psychology Today, American Scholar, Scientific Review,* and many others. An entry from *Readers' Guide to Periodical Literature* follows:

BRAIN STIMULATION IMPLANTS
Now, electronic 'eyes' for the blind [work of W. H. Dobelle]
O. Port. Il *Business Week* no3666 p56+ Ja 31 2000

■■■ **FIGURE 2.2**
From *Readers' Guide to Periodical Literature* showing subject, title, author, and publication data.

Make a bibliography entry for your research journal if it looks promising:

> Port, O. "Now, Electronic 'Eyes' for the Blind." <u>Business Week</u>
>   31 Jan. 2000: 56+.

Searching Indexes to Topics in the Humanities

Humanities Index (in print or online) catalogs 260 publications in several fields:

archaeology	folklore	performing arts
classical studies	history	philosophy
language and literature	literary	religion
area studies	political criticism	theology

MLA International Bibliography (in print and online) indexes most of the journals in language and literature studies. The printed versions are not kept up to date, so supplement the printed version with the electronic database, if available.

Abstracts of English Studies (in print or online) is an excellent place to begin research in literature studies.

Dissertation Abstracts International—A: Humanities and Social Sciences (in print and online) provides an index to the abstracts of all American dissertations. In the print version, look for issue No. 12, Part 11, of each volume, which contains the cumulated subject and author indexes for issues 1–12 of the volume's two sections.

Searching Indexes to Topics in the Social Sciences

Social Sciences Index (in print and online) indexes journal articles for 263 periodicals in these fields:

anthropology	geography	political
economics	law and criminology	science
environmental	medical science	psychology
science		sociology

Dissertation Abstracts International—A: Humanities and Social Sciences (see above).

Searching Indexes to Topics in the Physical Sciences

Applied Science and Technology Index (in print and online) for articles in chemistry, engineering, computer science, electronics, geology, mathematics, photography, physics, and related fields.

Biological and Agricultural Index (in print and online) for articles in biology, zoology, botany, agriculture, and related fields.

Dissertation Abstract International—B: Sciences and Engineering (in print and online) provides an index to the abstracts of all American dissertations in the fields of science and engineering. In the print version, look for issue No. 12, Part 11, of each volume, for it contains the cumulated subject and author indexes for Issues 1–12 of the volume's two sections.

Searching Indexes to Discipline-Specific Information

In addition to these general indexes, you should examine the indexes for your discipline as listed below in alphabetical order. Some are online by library access; others are found in printed versions in the library's reference room.

Art Index	*Chemical Abstracts*
Biological Abstracts	*Communication Abstracts*
Business Periodicals Index	*Computer Literature Index*

Economic Articles, Index of
Education Index
Engineering Index
Environment Abstracts
Geo Abstracts
Historical Abstracts
Literature, Cumulative Index
Mathematical Reviews
Music Index
Nursing and Allied Health

Philosopher's Index
Physical Education Index
Physics Abstracts
Political Science Abstracts,
   International
Psychological Abstracts
Religion Index One
Sociological Abstracts
Women's Studies Index

2f   Searching Biographies

Biographies of important people appear in books and articles, so you must use a variety of sources. The electronic book catalog (see section 2b) is a place to start with keywords, such as "biography + index," which lead to links to *Biography Index, Index to Literary Biography,* and many more. Otherwise, use the person's name as a keyword; for example, entering "Ben Franklin" produces a reference to, among many others, Cecil B. Currey's biography entitled *Ben Franklin: Patriot or Spy.*

In the library, examine these printed reference books:

Biography Index is a starting point for studies of famous persons. It leads to biographical information for people of all lands.

Current Biography Yearbook provides biographical sketches of notable people. Most articles are three to four pages long and, of importance, they include references to other sources at the end. This book is current, thorough, and international in scope.

Contemporary Authors provides a biographical guide for current writers in fiction, nonfiction, poetry, journalism, drama, motion pictures, television, and a few other fields. It describes most contemporary writers, giving biographical facts (including a current address and agent), sidelights, and, in many cases, an interview with the author. A bibliography of additional sources is usually included.

Dictionary of Literary Biography profiles thousands of writers in over 100 volumes under such titles as *American Humorists, Victorian Novelists,* and *American Newspaper Journalists.* A comprehensive index helps you locate the article on the author you are researching.

> ▌**HINT:** To find biographical reference works in a specific discipline, such as music or history, consult the library's electronic book catalog with a request such as "biographies of artists." This yields hyperlinks to *Who's Who in American Art* and similar works.

2g Searching Newspaper Indexes

Newspapers provide contemporary information. At the electronic catalog, ask for a particular newspaper and then use its archival search engine to find articles on your topic. For example, asking for the Nashville *Tennessean* provides the link to the newspaper. Then, entering a keyword such as "state lottery" provides access to articles in the current and previous editions of the *Tennessean*, as shown by this opening to an article:

Lawmaker: Home-schoolers shouldn't have tougher ACT mark
By DUREN CHEEK
Staff Writer

The **state**'s top lawyer was asked yesterday whether Tennessee's **lottery**-funded scholarship program is unconstitutional because it requires home-schooled students to meet higher standards than others entering college.

The request for an opinion came from **state** Rep. Glen Casada, R-College Grove, who said he thinks requiring home-schooled students to score a 23 on their ACT to qualify, while public school students must score only 19, is unfair and discriminatory.

"Proponents of a **lottery** did not mention discriminating against home-schooled students in the **lottery** debate last fall," said Casada, referring to the **lottery** referendum last November. Parents across the **state** were led to believe that students who met a certain criteria would receive a scholarship, period."

▌**FIGURE 2.3**
Opening paragraphs of an article in *The [Nashville] Tennessean*.

If your library's electronic catalog cannot access a specific newspaper you want, go to the Internet at **www.newspapers.com**. See page 41–42 for more information.

In your library, visit also the contemporary reading room, where you will find current issues of local and national newspapers on display for your reading pleasure or for research.

2h Searching the Indexes to Pamphlet Files

Librarians routinely clip items of interest from newspapers, bulletins, pamphlets, and miscellaneous materials and file them alphabetically by subject in loose-leaf folders. Make the pamphlet file a regular stop during preliminary investigation. Sometimes called the *vertical file,* it contains clippings on many topics, such as carpel tunnel syndrome, asbestos in the home, and medical care plans.

Two helpful pamphlets, online and in print, are SIRS and CQ Researcher. Social Issues Resources Series (SIRS) collects articles on special topics and reprints them as one unit; example topics are abortion, AIDS, prayer in schools, and pollution. With SIRS, you get ten or twelve articles readily available in one booklet.

The CQ Researcher, like SIRS, devotes one pamphlet to one topic, such as "energy and the environment." The pamphlet examines central issues on the topic, gives background information, shows a chronology of important events or processes, expresses an outlook, and provides an annotated bibliography.

HINT: For the correct citation forms to articles found in SIRS or CQ Researcher, see page 131.

2i   Searching Government Documents

All branches of the government publish and make available valuable material. At the library's list of available databases, click on GPO, which links you to the files of the Government Printing Office in Washington, DC. Then, as at other databases, enter your keyword, such as "SAT Scores," and the search engine will give you links to available documents. You can also search government documents on the Internet by entering **www.GPOAccess.gov** (see "Government," page 36, for additional information). Your library might also house printed copies of these valuable reference tools:

Monthly Catalog of United States Government Publications indexes all the documents published by the Government Printing Office.

Public Affairs Information Service Bulletin (PAIS) indexes articles and documents published by miscellaneous organizations. Its excellent index makes it a good starting point.

Congressional Record provides Senate and House bills, documents, and committee reports.

Public Papers of the Presidents of the United States is the publication of the Executive Branch, including not only the president's papers but also the documents of all members of the president's cabinet and various agencies.

U.S. Code is the publication of the Supreme Court, detailing decisions, codes, and other rulings.

> ■ **HINT:** See pages 133–134 for instructions in writing bibliography citations to the government.

2j Searching for Essays within Books

The *Essay and General Literature Index* (online and in print) helps you find essays hidden within anthologies. It indexes material of both a biographical and a critical nature. The essay listed in the example below might easily have been overlooked by any researcher.

King, Martin Luther, 1929–1968
Raboteau, A. J. Martin Luther King and the tradition of black religious protest. (*In* Religion and the life of the nation; ed. by R. A. Sherrill, p. 46–65).

You can get the call number for Sherrill's book through your library's electronic book catalog.

2k Building Your Research Journal

By now, you should have a collection of printed documents, photocopies, and downloaded files. It's important to keep your sources in order and clearly marked because you must cite authors and page numbers in your text, and you will need a Works Cited page that lists full information on each source. These may seem like obvious tasks, but reminders are helpful, and we have seen too many instances of students having to abandon perfectly good quotations because they could not find full data on the source for the Works Cited entry.

Build a computer folder. Create a folder on your hard drive for all of your computer files. Carry with you a floppy or zip drive for working at the labs and library. Each time you download an article, place it in this folder. As you gather more and more data and begin building an outline, you might create more than one folder.

Name each file precisely. Be descriptive in naming your files so you can identify the content after a few days. A file named Brown offers no clue to its contents. Instead, describe the contents—for example, BrownPesticidesandPets.

Organize a print folder. You need a notebook with sleeves for filing your written notes, printouts, and photocopies. This too should be organized along the lines of your outline.

Build a rough outline. Early on, write a rough outline to help you organize the mass of material you are gathering. It can also help identify topics needing more research. See page 3 for additional details.

Build a Works Cited file. As you discover sources that fit your outline or sources that you have slotted into your rough draft, enter them in your Works Cited file in alphabetical order. Thus, you accomplish a major task as you work your way through the project. This working bibliography should, at a minimum, contain the author's name, the title of the work, publication information, and a library call number if it's a book you have not yet examined. Shown below is an example, in MLA style, of one student's computer file in progress with three entries.

Works Cited

Dassman, Ray. "Voices." Interview of David Kupfer. Earth Island Journal 18 (2003): 48.

O'Malley, Martin, and John Bowman. "Selling Canada's Water." CBS News Online. June 2001. 9 Apr. 2003.

Postal, Sandra L. Last Oasis: Facing Water Scarcity. New York: Norton, 1992.

HINT: For other forms of bibliography entry, see the appropriate chapter for APA, CMS, and CSE styles in Chapters 10–12.

3

Searching the World Wide Web

Like a library, the Internet is a major source of research information. It makes available millions of computer files relating to every subject—articles, illustrations, sound and video clips, and raw data. However, the Internet cannot replace the library or field research. It offers the best and worst information, and requires careful evaluation. When reading an Internet article, always take time to judge its authority and veracity. This chapter will help you become an efficient searcher for academic information on the Internet.

3a Using a Search Engine

When you know your topic, perform a key search using the words you would like to find in the title, description, or text of an Internet source. For example, to find information on George W. Bush's environmental programs, enter the words *George W. Bush* and *environmental programs.* The search engine will direct you to a list of Web sites as shown, for example, by these three hyperlinks: <u>George W. Bush on Environment</u>, <u>George W. Bush's Policies and Plans</u>, <u>The Environmental Legacy of Governor George W. Bush</u>. You can then read the articles to determine if they relate to your research.

Using General Search Engines

About 100 excellent search engines are available. Some of the more popular are listed below. Many sites entice you with advertisements for various products, but they do an excellent job of directing you to a wide variety of sources. Experiment with them and select the one that works best for you.

Subject Directory Search Engines are compiled by humans and indexed to guide you to general areas that are then subdivided into narrower categories. Your choice of category controls the list.

About.com	**http://home.about.com/index.htm**
Go.network	**http://www.go.com**
Lycos	**http://www.lycos.com**
Yahoo!	**http://www.yahoo.com**

Robot-Driven Search Engines perform a keyword search by electronically scanning millions of Web pages. Your keyword phrase and Boolean operators control the list.

AltaVista	**http://altavista.digital.com/**
Excite	**http://www.excite.com**
Google	**http://www.google.com/**
Hotbot	**http://www.hotbot.com**
Webcrawler	**http://webcrawler.com**

Find one you prefer, but keep in mind that search engines are designed in different ways. AltaVista, for example, gives you a massive number of results from its more than 22 million Web pages. Yahoo!, on the other hand, is an edited site with directories and subdirectories.

Metasearch Engines simultaneously query about ten major search engines, such as those listed above, and provide you with a short, relevant set of results. You get fewer results than would appear at one of the major search engines. For example, "chocolate + children" produced 342,718 hits on AltaVista but only fifty on Mamma.com. A metasearch engine selects the first few listings from

CHECKLIST

Bookmarks

Most Web browser programs, such as Netscape, include a bookmark tool that enables you to save Web addresses for quick future access. For example, in Netscape, simply click on Bookmarks, then click on Add Bookmark. This will automatically add the current URL to the list of bookmarks. In Microsoft Internet Explorer, use the button bar marked Favorites to record an address. Bookmarks can easily be titled and organized so that you can make a bookmark file devoted to a list of sites related to your research paper. *Note:* If you are working at a university computer laboratory, do not add bookmarks to the hard drive. Instead, save the bookmarks to your disk by using Save As in the File menu of Netscape.

each of the search engines under the theory that each engine puts the most relevant results at the top of its list. This theory may or may not be true. Here are three metasearch engines:

Dogpile	**http://dogpile.com**
Mamma.com	**http://mamma.com**
Metacrawler.com	**http://metacrawler.com**

 ## 3b Using Search Engines Devoted to Academic Disciplines

Many search engines specialize in one area, such as Edweb (education studies) or Envirolink (environmental studies). The following list contains sites that may be helpful in launching your investigation of Internet resources.

Humanities
Art

The Parthenet **http://home.mtholyoke.edu/~klconner/ parthenet.html** This resource gives you information on ancient and classical art, the treasures of the Renaissance, nineteenth-century American works, Impressionism, and many other styles. It also links you with major museums and their collections.

World Wide Arts Resources **http://wwar.world-arts-resources. com** This site provides an artist index as well as an index to exhibits, festivals, meetings, and performances. Its search engine takes you to fine arts departments, online courses, syllabi, and art institutions.

History

Archiving Early America **http://earlyamerica.com** This site displays eighteenth-century documents in their original form for reading and downloading, such as the Bill of Rights and the speeches of Washington, Paine, Jefferson, and others.

Humanities Hub **http://www.gu.edu.au/gwis/hub.hom.html** This site provides resources in the humanities and social sciences with links to anthropology, architecture, cultural studies, film, gender studies, government, history, philosophy, sociology, and women.

Literature

The English Server **http://english-server.hss.cmu.edu** Carnegie Mellon University provides academic resources in the humanities, including drama, fiction, film, television, and history, plus calls for papers and a link for downloading freeware and shareware.

Literature Directory **http://web.syr.edu/~fjzwick/sites/lit.html** As the name says, this site provides a directory, with links, to specific works of literature.

Voice of the Shuttle **http://humanitas.ucsb.edu** For the literary scholar, this site gives a massive collection of bibliographies, textual criticism, newsgroups, and links to classical studies, history, philosophy, and related disciplines.

Philosophy

The American Philosophical Association **http://www.oxy.edu/apa.html** This site provides articles, bibliographies, software, a bulletin board, a gopher server, and links to other philosophy sites containing college courses, journals, texts, and newsletters.

Episteme Links: Philosophy Resources on the Internet **http://www.epistemelinks.com/** This site offers links to biographies, philosophical movements, and full-text works.

HINT: If you have problems accessing a particular site, try truncating the address by cutting items from the end. For example, cut **http://www.emory.edu/WHSC/ medweb.medlibs.html** to **http://www.emory.edu**. At this main page of the Web site, you can search for whatever file you need.

Religion

Comparative Religion **http://weber.u.washington.edu/~madin** This comprehensive site gives references and resources to all religions, religious studies, and religious organizations.

Vanderbilt Divinity School **http://www.library.vanderbilt.edu/divinity/homelib.html** This source gives references to and interpretations of the Bible, links to other religious Web sites, and online journals, such as *Biblical Archaeologist.*

Social Sciences

Business

All Business Network **http://www.all-biz.com** This site provides a search engine to businesses with relevant information for the following—newsletters, organizations, newsgroups, and magazines.

Finance: The World Wide Web Virtual Library **http://www.cob.ohio-state.edu/dept/fin/overview.html** The Finance Department of Ohio State University has established a site that links to hundreds of articles and resource materials on banks, insurers, market news, jobs, and miscellaneous data for students.

Nijenrode Business Webserver **http://www.nijenrode.nl/nbr/ index.html** This site serves primarily students and faculty at business schools with a search engine that finds news, business journals, and career opportunities in accounting, banking, finance, marketing, and related fields.

Communication

Communication Resources on the Web **http://alnilam.ucs.indiana. edu:1027/sources/comm.html** This large database takes you to resources and Web sites on associations, book reviews, bibliographies, libraries, media, information science programs, and university departments of communication.

Education

Educom **http://educom.edu** This site has full-text online articles with a focus on educational technology in its *Educom Review,* a focus on information technology in *Edupage,* and general news from *Educom Update.*

Edweb **http://edweb.cnidr.org:90** This site focuses on educational issues and resource materials for grades K–12 with articles on Web education, history, and resources.

ERIC (Educational Resource and Information Center) **http:// ericir.syr.edu/ithome** ERIC is considered the primary source of research information for most educators. It contains about 1 million documents, available by keyword search, on all aspects of teaching and learning, lesson plans, administration, bibliographies, and almost any topic related to the classroom.

Government

Fedworld **http:// www.fedworld.gov** This site gives links to the Web sites of government departments, including the Internal Revenue Service, as well as lists of free catalogs.

Library of Congress **http://www.lcweb.loc.gov** This site provides the Library of Congress catalog online for books by author, subject, and title. It also links to historical collections and research tools, such as Thomas, which provides access to congressional legislation.

White House Web **http://www.whitehouse.gov** This site provides a graphical tour, messages from the President and the Vice President, and accounts of life at the White House. Visitors to this site can even leave a message for the President in the guest book.

Political Science

Political Science Resources on the Web **http://www.lib.umich.edu/ libhome/Documents.center/polisci.html** This site at the University of Michigan is a vast data file on government information—local, state, federal, foreign, and international. It is a good site for political theory and international relations, with links to dissertations, periodicals, reference sources, university courses, and other social science information.

Psychology

PsycINFO **http://www.apa.org/psycinfo** The American Psychological Association (APA) maintains this excellent site for current and archival information in associated disciplines.

Psych Web **http://www.gasou.edu/psychweb/psychweb. htm#top** This site features a collection of articles from *Psychiatric Times,* reports from the National Institute of Health, information from universities, and links to psychology journals and other sites on the Internet. It includes, online, Freud's *Interpretation of Dreams.*

Sociology

Social Science Information Gateway (SOSIG) **http://sosig.esrc. bris.ac.uk/Welcome.html#socialsciences** The SOSIG site allows a keyword search that yields an alphabetical list of many Web sites.

Sociology **http://hakatai.mcli.dist.maricopa.edu/smc/ml/ sociology.html** This site gives access to hundreds of sites that provide articles and resource materials on almost all aspects of sociology.

Women's Studies

The Women's Resource Project **http://sunsite.unc.edu/cheryb/ women** This site links to libraries on the Web that have collections on women's studies. It also has links to women's programs and women's resources on the Web.

Women's Studies Resources **http://www.lib.umd.edu/ETC/SUBR/ resources.women-studies.html** This site features a search engine for a keyword search of women's issues and provides directories to bibliographies, classic texts, references, course syllabi from various universities, and gateways to several other Web sites.

Sciences

Astronomy

American Astronomical Society **http://www.aas.org** This site features the *Astrophysical Journal,* which provides articles, reviews, and educational information. The site also links to other astronomy Web sites.

The Universe at Our Doorstep **http://neptune.cgy.oanet.comp** This site links to NASA programs such as the space station, the shuttle program, and Project Galileo. It provides maps of the planets, views of Earth from many angles, and plenty of planetary information.

Computer and Internet Technology

Computer Science **http://library.albany.edu/subjects/csci.htm** This site is a good starting point for students because it provides numerous links to resources in the computer disciplines.

Internet Society (ISOC) **http://www.isoc.org/indextxt.html** This site is supported by the companies, agencies, and foundations that launched the Internet and that keep it functioning. It gives vital information through articles from the *ISOC Forum* newsletter.

Virtual Computer Library **http://www.utexas.edu/computer/ucl** This site gives access to academic computing centers at the major universities along with books, articles, and bibliographies.

Environmental Science

Envirolink **http://envirolink.org** This site has a search engine that allows access to environmental articles, photographs, action alerts, organizations, and additional Web sources.

The Virtual Library of Ecology and Biodiversity **http://conbio.net/VL/welcome.cfm** Sponsored by the Center for Conservation Biology, this site provides valuable links to Web sites in categories such as endangered species, global sustainability, and pollution.

General Science

The Academy of Natural Sciences **http://www.acnatsci.org/links.html** This site links to hundreds of articles and resource materials on various issues and topics in the natural sciences.

BIOSIS **http://www.biosis.org/** This site provides searchable databases in biology and life sciences and serves as an excellent resource for students wishing to conduct scientific research.

National Academy of Sciences **http://www.nas.edu** This comprehensive site combines the resources of the National Academy of

Engineering, the Institute of Medicine, and the National Research Council. It focuses on math and science education and offers links to scientific societies.

Health and Medicine

Global Health Network **http://www.healthnet.org/MGS/MGS.html** This online journal provides articles on environmental destruction, overpopulation, infectious diseases, the consequences of war, and, in general, the health of the globe. It offers links to other journals, newsletters, and government documents that explore environmental issues.

Medweb: Medical Libraries **http://www.emory.edu/WHSC/medweb.medlibs.html** Emory University provides a site that connects with medical libraries and their storehouses of information. It also gives links to other health-related Web sites.

National Institutes of Health **http://www.nih.gov** NIH leads the nation in medical research, so this site provides substantive information on numerous topics, from cancer and diabetes to malpractice and medical ethics. It provides links to online journals for the most recent news in medical science.

HINT: You can quickly build a bibliography on the Internet in two ways: (1) At a search engine such as AltaVista, enter a descriptive phrase such as *child abuse bibliographies,* and (2) Use the search engines of Amazon **www.amazon.com** and Barnes and Noble **www.bn.com** to gather a list of books currently in print. Then, find the books at your library.

3c   Accessing Online Sources

Several types of sources are available, and you should use more than one type in your research.

Internet Home Pages

You can locate home pages for individuals, institutions, and organizations by using a search engine such as Yahoo! and AltaVista (see page 33). Type in a person's name or the name of an organization, such as the American Psychological Association, to get a link to the site **http://www.apa.org/**. The site's home page, in turn, provides links, a directory, an index, or an internal search engine that will take you quickly to specific material.

Internet Articles on the Web

A search engine will direct you to many articles on the Web, some isolated without documentation and credentials and others that list the author as well as the association to which the author belongs. For example, a search for *child care centers* will produce local sites such as Apple Tree Family Child Care. Private sites like these will add local knowledge to your research. Adding another relevant term, such as *child care regulations,* will take you to state and national sites such as the National Resource Center for Health and Safety in Child Care.

> **HINT:** An Internet article that contains only a title and the URL cannot be properly documented and should be avoided.

Journal Articles on the Web

The Internet supplies journal articles of two types: (1) articles in online journals designed and published only on the Web, and (2) reproductions of articles that have appeared in printed journals. Find them in three ways.

- Using your favorite search engine, enter a keyword phrase for journals plus the name of your subject. For example, one student, using AltaVista, entered a keyword search for *journals+fitness* and found links to twenty journals devoted to fitness, including *Health Page, Excite Health,* and *Physical Education.*
- Access a search engine's subject directory. In Yahoo!, for example, one student selected Social Science from the key directory, clicked on Sociology, clicked on Journals, and accessed links to several online journals, including *Sociological Research Online* and *Edge: The E-Journal of Intercultural Relations.*
- If you already know the name of a journal, go to your favorite search engine to make a keyword query such as *Psycholoquy,* a social science journal.

Note: Some journals furnish an abstract but require a fee for access to the full text.

> **HINT:** Remember that abstracts may not accurately represent the full article. In fact, some abstracts are not written by the author at all but by an editorial staff. Resist the desire to copy quotations from the abstract; instead, write a paraphrase or, better, find the full text and cite from it.

Magazine Articles on the Web

The Internet supplies magazine articles of two types. Some appear in original online magazines designed and published only on the Web. Others are reproductions of articles that have appeared in printed magazines. Several directories exist for finding magazine articles:

NewsDirectory.com **http://www.ecola.com/new/** This site takes you to magazine home pages, where you can search that magazine's archives. A search for *current events,* for example, will send you to *Atlantic Monthly* **theatlantic.com,** *Harper's* **harpers.org,** and *Newsweek* **Newsweek.com.**

Electric Library **http://www.elibrary.com/** This Web site has a subscription-based search engine with links to 17 million documents in newspapers, magazines, and news services. You can get free access for seven days. Remember to cancel your membership after finishing your research or charges will accrue.

Pathfinder **http://pathfinder.com/** This site gives free access to *Time* magazine and has a good search engine with links to thousands of archival articles.

ZD Net **http://www.zdnet.com/** This site provides excellent access to industry-oriented articles on banking, electronics, computers, and management. You can receive two weeks of free access before charges begin to accrue.

You can also access online magazines through a search engine's directory. For example, using AltaVista, one student clicked on Health and Fitness in the subject directory of the home page, clicked next on Publications and then Magazines. The result was a list of forty magazines devoted to various aspects of health and fitness, such as *Healthology* and *The Black Health Net.*

News Sources

Most major news organizations maintain Internet sites. Consult one of these:

CNN Interactive **http://www.cnn.com** This search engine takes you quickly, without cost, to transcripts of CNN broadcasts, making it a good source for research in current events.

C-SPAN Online **http://www.c-span.org** This site emphasizes public affairs and offers both a directory and a search engine with links to transcripts. It is a valuable source for research in public affairs, government, and political science.

National Public Radio Online **http://www.npr.org** This site provides audio articles via RealPlayer or some other audio engine. Be prepared to take careful notes.

The *New York Times* on the Web **http://www.nytimes.com** You can read recent articles for free. However, if you search the 365-day archive, have your credit card ready. Articles cost $2.50. After purchase, they appear on the monitor for printing or downloading.

USA Today DeskTopNews **http://www.usatoday.com** This site's rapid search engine provides information about current events.

U.S. News Online **http://www.usnews.com** This site has a fast search engine and provides free, in-depth articles on current political and social issues.

The *Washington Times* **http://www.washingtontimes.com/** This site is a good source of up-to-the-minute political news.

The *CQ Weekly* **http://library.cq.com** This magazine keeps tabs on congressional activities in Washington.

To find additional newspapers, search **www.newspapers.com**. Your college library may also provide Lexis-Nexis, which searches online news sources for you.

HINT: Document Internet sources to avoid the appearance of citing from the printed version. Major differences often exist between the same article in *USA Today* and in *USA Today* DeskTopNews.

Books on the Web

One of the best sources of full-text, online books is the Online Books Page at the University of Pennsylvania: **http://digital.library.upenn.edu/books/**. This site indexes books by author, title, and subject. Its search engine takes you quickly to the full text of Thomas Hardy's *A Pair of Blue Eyes* or Linnea Hendrickson's *Children's Literature: A Guide to the Criticism.* This site adds new textual material almost every day, so consult it first. Understand, however, that contemporary books, still under copyright protection, are not included. That is, you can freely download an Oscar Wilde novel but not one by contemporary writer J. K. Rowling. Here are a few additional sites:

Bartleby.com	**http://www.bartleby.com**
Internet Classics Archive	**http://classics.mit.edu**

Project Gutenberg	**http://promo.net/pg/**
Bibliomania	**http://www.bibliomania.com**
Education Planet	**http://educationplanet.com**
American Literary Classics	**http://www.americanliterature.com**

There are many more; in a search engine, use a keyword request for *full-text books*.

E-mail Discussion Groups

Discussion groups correspond by e-mail on a central topic. For example, your literature professor might ask everybody in the class to join an e-mail discussion group on Victorian literature. To participate, you must have an e-mail address and subscribe to the list. In an online class using Blackboard, for instance, special forums can be designated that request the response of all members in the class. Your participation may contribute to your final grade.

Real-time chatting is also available through immediate messages on the Internet or with members of chat groups. However, we discourage the use of chat commentary for your research. Even though Yahoo!, AltaVista, AOL, and other servers offer access to chat groups, you cannot quote people with fictional usernames and no credentials.

Archives

In addition to searching the archives via your library's electronic catalog (see pages 15–17), you can find documents on the Internet.

1. For archival research in government documents, see Library of Congress **http://www.loc.gov**. This site allows you to search by word, phrase, name, title, series, and number. It provides special features such as an American Memory Home Page, full-text legislative information, and exhibitions such as the drafts of Lincoln's Gettysburg Address.

2. Go to an edited search engine such as Yahoo! to find results quickly. For example, requesting *Native American literature+archives* produced such links as American native press archives, Native American History Archive, Native Americans and the Environment, Indigenous Peoples' Literature, and Sayings of Chief Joseph.

3. Go to a metasearch engine such as **dogpile.com** and make a request such as *Native American literature+archives*. The engine will list such sites as Reference Works and Research Material for Native American Studies **http://www.stanford.edu**.

There you would find archives entitled Native American Studies Encyclopedias and Handbooks, Native American Studies Bibliographies, Native American Studies Periodical Indexes, and Native American Biography Resources.

4. Use the directory and subdirectories of a search engine to move deeper and deeper into the files. Remember, this tracing goes quickly. Here is an example that shows how the directories can carry you rather swiftly from a browser's main page to archives of ancient warfare: AltaVista: Society > History > By Time Period > Ancient > Warfare in the Ancient World > The Legend of the Trojan War.

C H E C K L I S T

Evaluating Internet Sources

- Prefer the .edu and .org sites. Usually these are domains developed by an educational institution, such as Ohio State University, or by a professional organization, such as the American Psychological Association. The .gov (government) and .mil (military) sites usually have reliable materials.

- The .com (commercial) sites are suspect for several reasons: (1) They sell advertising space, (2) They often charge for access to their files, and (3) They can be ISP (Internet Service Providers) sites where people pay to post material that has not been edited and subjected to peer review.

- What is the date? References in the sciences demand a date because research grows old quickly. For the same reason, look for the date when the Web information was last revised.

- Look for the professional affiliation of the writer, which you will find in the opening credits or an e-mail address. Ask this question: Is the writer affiliated with a professional organization? Information should be included in the opening credit. An e-mail address might also show academic affiliation. Is contact information for the author or sponsoring organization included in the document?

Other ways to investigate the credibility of a writer are searching for the writer's home page and looking on Amazon.com for a list of his or her books.

- Can you identify the target audience? What does it tell you about the purpose of the Web site? Remember, the research generally calls for Web sites that appeal to the intellectual person.

- What bias colors the Web site? *Note:* There is always a bias of some sort because even academic sites show bias toward, for example, the grandeur of Greek philosophy, the brilliance of the Allied Forces in World War II, or the artistry of Picasso's Blue period.

- Look at the end of Internet articles for a bibliography of sources that indicate the scholarly nature of the writer's work.

- Treat e-mail as mail, not as a scholarly source. Academic discussion groups may sometimes contain valuable information, but use it only if you know the source.

- Do not cite from chat forums where fictitious usernames are common.

- Hypertext links to educational sites serve as an academic bibliography to reliable sources. However, if the site gives hypertext links to commercial sites or if spam floods the screen, abandon the site and do not quote from it.

- Learn to distinguish among types of Web sites such as advocacy pages, personal home pages, informational pages, and business and marketing pages. One site provides several evaluation techniques that might prove helpful: **http://www2.widener.edu/Wolfgram-Memorial-Library/webevaluation/webeval.htm**.

- Your skills in critical reading and thinking can usually determine the validity of a site. For more information on critical reading, visit this site: **http://www.library.ucla.edu/libraries/college/help/critical/**.

4

Field Research: Collecting Data outside the Library

The human species is distinguished by its ability to examine the world systematically and create pioneers for the millennium, such as computer technicians, microsurgeons, and nuclear engineers. You may become one of them. Each discipline has different expectations in its methods of inquiry and presentation. This chapter introduces you to types of field research and the results you might expect.

4a   Conducting Research within a Discipline

Some disciplines, more than others, require you to work in the laboratory or the field, not just the library. Attitudes and methods differ among the social, physical, and applied sciences, and those three differ in many ways from the attitudes and methods of humanists.

The Social Scientists

Social scientists work from the assumption that behavior can be observed, tested, and catalogued by observation and experimental testing. Professionals perform thousands of experiments every month. They research stress in the workplace, study the effects of birth order on the youngest child, and develop testing mechanisms, such as the Scholastic Aptitude Test (SAT). As a student in the social sciences, you are asked to perform similar but less exhaustive studies, such as the typing mannerisms of students composing on a computer. If your topic examines any aspect of human behavior (for example, road rage on campus streets), prepare to go into the field for some aspects of your research.

The Physical Scientists

Physical scientists wish to discover, define, and explain the natural world. They operate under the assumption that we can know precise data on flora and fauna, geological formations, the various species of animals, and so forth. You may be asked to join a field expedition to catalog one type of fern, to test the water conditions at a local lake, or to locate sinkholes in a confined area. Laboratory experimentation is also a regular activity of scientists, so any experiments you conduct should be recorded in a lab notebook and may become significant to your written reports. If your topic examines the natural world in some way—for example, the growing deer population in the Governor Oaks subdivision—field research may be useful.

The Applied Scientists

Applied scientists *apply* scientific knowledge to make life more efficient, enduring, and comfortable. By means of mathematical formulas and cutting-edge technology, they launch spaceships to encircle the globe, find new ways to repair broken bones, and discover better methods of movie animation. You, too, can participate in such experiments by designing access facilities for students with wheelchairs (for example, should doors open out or open in?), investigating systems to measure the force of lightning strikes, or examining ways to increase the weight of beef cattle. It is not unusual today for undergraduate students to apply computer knowledge to the creation of new programs, even new software and hardware. If your research involves application of scientific information, researching in the field may help you formulate your ideas.

The Humanists

Humanists in the fine arts, literature, history, religion, and philosophy have a distinctive approach to knowledge. While scientists usually investigate a small piece of data and its meaning, humanists examine an entire work of art (Verdi's opera *Rigoletto*), a period of history (the Great Depression), or a philosophical theory (existentialism). Humanists usually accept a poem or painting as a valid entity and search it subjectively for what it means to human experience. However, that does not preclude humanists from conducting field research. For example, a student might go to England to retrace the route of late medieval pilgrims to Canterbury, as such a trip might shed new light on Chaucer's poetry. In another instance, a student's field trip to Jackson, Mississippi, might enlighten the scholar on the fiction of Eudora Welty. Conducting archival research on manuscript materials could take you into unknown territory. Your work with a writer living in your locality may prompt you to seek a personal interview, and correspondence with writers and historians is standard fare in humanist research. Thus, if your research in history, religion, or the arts offers the opportunity for field research, add it to your research program.

4b Investigating Local Sources

Interviewing Knowledgeable People

Talk to persons who have experience with your subject. Personal interviews can elicit valuable in-depth information. They provide information that few others have. Look to organizations for experienced persons. For example, a student writing on a folklore topic might contact the county historian, a senior citizens organization, or a local historical society. If necessary, the student could post a notice soliciting help: "I am writing a study of local folklore. Wanted: People who have a knowledge of regional tales." Another way to accomplish this task is to request information from an e-mail discussion group, which will bring responses from several persons (see pages 5 and 43 for details).

Follow a few general guidelines. Set up your appointments in advance. Consult with persons knowledgeable about your topic. If possible, talk to several people to get a fair assessment. A telephone interview is acceptable, as is e-mail correspondence. Be courteous and on time for interviews. Be prepared with a set of focused, relevant questions. For accuracy and if permitted by the person being interviewed, record the session on audiotape or videotape. Double-check direct quotations with the interviewee or the tape. Get permission before citing a person by name or quoting the person's exact words. Handle private and public papers with great care, and send participants a copy of your report along with a thank-you note. Make a bibliography entry just as you would for a book:

Thornbright, Mattie Sue. Personal interview. 15 Jan. 2004.

Writing Letters and Corresponding by E-mail

Correspondence provides a written record for research. Write a letter asking pointed questions that will elicit relevant responses. Tell the person who you are, what you are attempting to do, and why you are writing to him or her.

Gena Messersmith
12 Morningside Road
Clarksville, TN

Ms. Rachel G. Warren, Principal
Sango High School
Clarksville, TN

Dear Ms. Warren:
I am a college student conducting research into methods for
handling hyperactive children in the public school setting. I am
surveying each elementary school principal in the county. I have
contacted the central office also, but I wished to have perspectives from those of you on the front lines. I have a child with
ADHD, so I have a personal as well as a scholarly reason for this
research. I could ask specific questions on policy, but I have got-
ten that from the central office. What I would like from you is
a brief paragraph that describes your policy and procedure
when one of your teachers reports a hyperactive child. In particular, do you endorse the use of medication for calming the
child with ADHD? May I quote you in my report? I will honor
any request to withhold your name.
    I have enclosed a self-addressed, stamped envelope for your
convenience. You may e-mail me at messersmithg@apsu.edu.
    Sincerely,
    Gena Messersmith

This letter makes a fairly specific request for a minimum amount of
information. It does not require an expansive reply. If Gena Messersmith
uses a quotation from the reply and if she has permission from the interviewee, she can provide a bibliography entry on her Works Cited page.

Warren, Rachel G. Principal of Sango High School,
    Clarksville, TN. E-mail to the author. 5 Apr. 2004.

If Messersmith decides to build a table or graph from replies
received, she must document the survey as shown on page 52.

Reading Personal Papers

    Search for letters, diaries, manuscripts, family histories, and other
personal materials that might contribute to your study. The city
library may house private collections, and the public librarian might
help you contact the county historian and other private citizens who
have important documents. Obviously, handling private papers must
be done with the utmost decorum and care. Make a bibliography
entry for such materials.

Joplin, Lester. "Notes on Robert Penn Warren." Unpublished
    paper. Nashville, 1997.

Attending Lectures and Public Addresses

Watch bulletin boards and the newspaper for a public speaker who may contribute to your research. At the lecture, take careful notes, and if the speaker makes one available, secure a copy of the lecture or speech. If you want to use your equipment to make an audiotape or videotape of a speech, courtesy demands that you seek permission. Remember, too, that many lectures, reproduced on video, are available in the library or in departmental files. Always make a bibliography entry for any words or ideas you use.

> Petty-Rathbone, Virginia. "Edgar Allan Poe and the Image of Ulalume." Lecture. Heard Library, Vanderbilt U., 2000.

Investigating Government Documents

Documents are available at four levels of government: city, county, state, and federal. As a constituent, you are entitled to examine a wide assortment of records on file at various agencies. If your topic demands it, you may contact the mayor's office, attend and take notes at a meeting of the county commissioners, or search for documents in the archives of the state or federal government.

City and County Government

Visit the courthouse or county clerk's office to find facts on elections, censuses, marriages, births, and deaths as well as census data. These archives include wills, tax rolls, military assignments, deeds to property, and much more. A trip to the local courthouse can help you trace the history of the land and its people.

State Government

Contact a state office that relates to your research, such as Consumer Affairs (which provides general information), Public Service Commission (which regulates public utilities such as the telephone company), or the Department of Human Services (which administers social and welfare services). The names of these agencies may vary from state to state. Each state has an archival storehouse and makes its records available for public review.

Federal Government

Your United States senator or representative can send you booklets printed by the Government Printing Office (GPO). A list of these materials, many of which are free, appears on the GPO Web site **www.GPOAccess.gov**. In addition, you can gain access to the National Archives Building in Washington, DC, or to one of the regional branches in Atlanta, Boston, Chicago, Denver, Fort Worth, Kansas City, Los Angeles, New York, Philadelphia, or Seattle. Their archives contain court records and government documents that you can review in two books: *Guide to the National Archives of the United States* and *Select List of Publications of the National Archives and Record Service.* You can view some documents on microfilm if you consult the *Catalog of National Archives Microfilm Publications.*

 ## Examining Audiovisual Materials, Television, and Radio

Important data can be found in audiovisual materials. You can find these both on and off campus. Consult such guides as *Educators Guide* (film, film strips, and tapes), *Media Review Digest* (nonprint materials), *Video Source Book* (video catalog), *The Film File,* or *International Index to Recorded Poetry.* Television, with its many channels, such as The History Channel, offers invaluable data. With a VCR, you can record a program for detailed examination. The Internet houses articles on almost every conceivable topic. As for other sources, write bibliography entries for any materials that have merit and contribute to your paper.

"Nutrition and AIDS." Narr. Carolyn O'Neil. CNN.
    12 Jan. 1997.

When using media sources, watch closely the opening and closing credits to capture the necessary data for your bibliography entry. The format is explained on pages 138–39. As with the personal interview, be scrupulously accurate in taking notes. Citations may refer to a performer, director, or narrator, depending on the focus of your study. It is best to write direct quotations because paraphrases of television commentary can unintentionally be distorted by bias. Always scrutinize material taken from an Internet site (see pages 44–45 for a checklist of ways to evaluate Internet articles).

 ## Conducting a Survey with a Questionnaire

Questionnaires can produce current, firsthand data that you can tabulate and analyze. To achieve meaningful results, you must survey randomly with regard to age, sex, race, education, income, residence, and other factors. Bias can creep into the questionnaire unless you remain objective. Use a formal survey only if you are experienced with tests and measurements and statistical analysis or when you have an instructor who will help you with the instrument. Be advised that most schools have a Human Subjects Committee that sets guidelines, draws up consent forms, and requires anonymity of participants for information-gathering that might be intrusive. An informal survey gathered in the hallways of campus buildings lacks credibility in the research paper. If you build a table or graph from the results, see page 199 for an example and instructions.

Surveys usually depend on *quantitative* methodologies, which produce numerical data. That is, the questionnaire results are tallied to reflect campus crime rates, parking slots for students, or the shifts in student population in off-campus housing. In some cases a survey depends on *qualitative* methodologies; these assess answers to questions on social issues, such as the number of biased words in a history text, the reasons for marijuana use, or levels of hyperactivity in a test group of children.

Label your survey in the bibliography entry:

Mason, Valerie, and Sarah Mossman. "Child Care
    Arrangements of Parents Who Attend College."
    Questionnaire. Knoxville: U of Tennessee, 2004.

Keep the questionnaire short, clear, and focused on your topic. Questions must be unbiased. Ask your professor to review the instrument before using it. Design your questionnaire for a quick response to a scale ("Choose A, B, or C"), a ranking (first choice, second choice, and so on), or fill-in blanks. You should also arrange for an easy return of the questionnaire by providing a self-addressed stamped envelope or by allowing respondents to send in their completed questionnaires by e-mail.

Tabulate the responses objectively. Present the results—positive or negative—as well as a sample questionnaire in the appendix to your paper. While results that deny your hypothesis may not support the outcome you desire, they still have value.

4e Conducting Experiments, Tests, and Observation

Empirical research, performed in a laboratory or in the field, can determine why and how things exist, function, or interact with one another. Your paper will explain your methods and findings in pursuit of a hypothesis or theory. An experiment thereby becomes primary evidence for your paper.

Observation occurs generally in the field, which might be a child care center, a movie theater, a parking lot, or the counter of a McDonald's restaurant. The field is anywhere you can observe, count, and record behavior, patterns, and systems. It can be testing the water in a stream or observing the nesting patterns of deer. Retail merchandisers conduct studies to observe buying habits. A basketball coach might gather and analyze data on shot selections by members of his team. Gathering data is a way of life for television executives, politicians, and thousands of marketing professionals.

A *case study* is a formal report based on your observation of a human subject. For example, you might examine patterns of behavior to build a profile, or you can base your case study on biographical data, interviews, tests, and observation. You might observe and interview an older person with dementia; that would be a case study and evidence for your research paper. Each discipline has its own standards for properly conducting a case study. You should not examine any subject without the guidance and approval of your instructor. For an example of a case study, see pages 158–66 of the paper by Valerie Nesbitt-Hall.

Most experiments and observations begin with a *hypothesis,* which is similar to a thesis sentence (see pages 8–11). The hypothesis is a statement assumed to be true for the purpose of investigation. *Hummingbirds live as extended families governed by a patriarch* is a hypothesis for which data are needed to prove its validity. *The majority of people will not correct the poor grammar of a speaker* is a hypothesis for which testing and observation must be conducted to prove its validity.

You can begin observation without a hypothesis and let the results lead you to the implications. Shown below is one student's double-entry format used to record observation on the left and commentary on the right. This is a limited example of field notes.

Record:	*Response:*
Day 1	
10-minute session at window, 3 hummingbirds fighting over the feeder	Is the male chasing away the female, or is the female the aggressor?
Day 2	
10-minute session at window, saw 8 single hummingbirds at feeder #1 and 1 guarding feeder #2 by chasing others away.	I did some research, and the red-throated male is the one that's aggressive.

Generally, a report on an experiment or observation follows a format that provides four distinct parts: introduction, method, results, and discussion. These four divisions of the scientific report are discussed fully in section 7a, page 79.

CHECKLIST

Conducting an Experiment or Observation

- Express clearly your hypothesis in the introduction.
- Provide a review of the literature if necessary for establishing an academic background for the work.
- Explain your design for the study—lab experiment, observation, or the collection of raw data in the field.
- Design the work for maximum respect to your subjects. In that regard, you may find it necessary to get approval for your research from a governing board.
- For the results section, maintain careful records and accurate data. Don't let your expectations influence the results.
- In your conclusion, discuss your findings and any implications to be drawn.

5

Understanding and Avoiding Plagiarism

This chapter defines plagiarism, explores the ethical standards for writing in an academic environment, and provides examples of the worst and best of citations. Plus, we must face the newest problem: The Internet makes it easy to copy and download material and paste it into a paper—which in itself is not a problem *unless* you fail to acknowledge the source.

Intellectual property has value. If you write a song, you have a right to protect your interests. Thus, the purpose of this chapter is to explore with you the ethics of research writing, especially about these matters:

- Using sources to enhance your credibility
- Using sources to place a citation in its proper context
- Honoring property rights
- Avoiding plagiarism
- Honoring and crediting sources in online course work

5a Using Sources to Enhance Your Credibility

What some students fail to realize is that citing a source in their papers, even the short ones, signals something special and positive to readers—that the student has researched the topic, explored the literature about it, and has the expertise to share it. By announcing clearly the name of a source, the writer reveals the scope of his or her critical reading in the literature, as shown in these notes by one student:

Sandra Postel says water is "a living system that drives the workings of a natural world we depend on" (19). Postel declares: "A new water era has begun" (24). She indicates that the great prairies of the world will dry up, including

America's. Hey, when folks in America notice the drought, then maybe something will happen. Let's watch what happens when Texas goes dry as a bone.

These notes give clear evidence of the writer's investigation into the subject, and they enhance the student's image as a researcher. This student will receive credit for naming and quoting the source. The opposite, *plagiarism*, might get the student into trouble, as we discuss in section 5d.

5b Identifying Bias in a Source

You show integrity in your use of sources by identifying any bias expressed by a writer or implied by the political stance of a magazine. For example, if you are writing about federal aid to farmers, you will find different opinions in a farmer's magazine and a journal that promotes itself as a watchdog to federal spending. One is an advocate and the other a vocal opponent. You may quote these sources, but only if you identify them carefully. Let us examine the problem faced by one student. Student Jamie Johnston, in researching articles on savagery in prehistoric wars, found articles of interest and positioned them in his paper with a description of the sources, as shown in this passage that carefully identifies exactly what the authority claims. Notice especially the final sentence by Johnston. You will find the research paper on pages 175–80.

> The evidence offers several assertions. Ben Harder has reported on the work of one forensic anthropologist, John Verano, who had investigated a series of "grisly executions" in the valley of Peru during the Moche civilization (cited in Harder). Victims "were apparently skinned alive. Others were drained of blood, decapitated, or bound tightly and left to be eaten by vultures" (cited in Harder). Verano has the proof of the executions, but not the reason, although his speculations center on religious ceremonies.

You owe your readers this favor: Examine articles, especially those in magazines and on the Internet, for special interests, opinionated speculation, or an absence of credentials by the writer. Be wary of Web sites without an academic or government sponsor. Refer to Chapter 3, which lists the most reliable databases.

5c Honoring Property Rights

If you invent a new piece of equipment or a child's toy, you can get a patent that protects your invention. You now own it. If you own a company, you can register a symbol that serves as a trademark for the products produced. You own the trademark. In like manner, if you write a set of poems and publish them in a chapbook, you own the poems. Others must seek your permission before they can reproduce the poems, just as others must buy your trademark or pay to produce your toy.

The principle behind the copyright law is relatively simple. Copyright begins at the time a creative work is recorded in some tangible form—a written document, a drawing, a tape recording. It does not depend on a legal registration with the copyright office in Washington, DC, although published works are usually registered. The moment you express yourself creatively on paper, in a song, on a canvas, that expression is your intellectual property. You have a vested interest in any profits made from the distribution of your work. For that reason, songwriters, cartoonists, fiction writers, and other artists guard their work and do not want it disseminated without compensation.

Scholarly work rarely involves direct compensation, but recognition is certainly an important need. We provide recognition by means of in-text citations and bibliography entries. As a student, you may use copyrighted material in your research paper under a doctrine of *fair use* as described in the U.S. Code, which says:

> The fair use of a copyrighted work . . . for purposes such as criticism, comment, news reporting, teaching (including multiple copies for classroom use), scholarship, or research is not an infringement of copyright.

Thus, as long as you borrow for educational purposes, such as a paper to be read by your instructor, you should not be concerned about violating the copyright law, as long as you provide documentation. However, if you decide to *publish* your research paper on a Web site, then new considerations come into play and you should seek the advice of your instructor.

5d Avoiding Plagiarism

Write most of the paper yourself. First, develop personal notes full of your own ideas on a topic. Discover how you feel about the issue. Then, rather than copying sources one after another, express your own ideas at the beginning of paragraphs and then synthesize the ideas of others by using summary, paraphrase, and quotation. Rethink and reconsider ideas you gathered in your reading, make meaningful connections, and, when you refer to a specific source—as you inevitably will—give it credit.

Plagiarism is offering the words or ideas of another person as one's own. Major violations, which can bring failure in the course or expulsion from school, are:

- The use of another student's work
- The purchase of a canned research paper
- Copying passages into your paper without documentation
- Copying a key, well-worded phrase without documentation
- Placing specific ideas of others in your own words without documentation

These instances represent deliberate attempts to deceive. Closely related, but not technically plagiarism, is the fabrication of information—that is, making information up. Some newspaper reporters have lost their jobs because of such fabrication.

A gray area in plagiarism is simply student carelessness—for example, failure to enclose quoted material within quotation marks even though you provide an in-text citation, or a paraphrase that never quite becomes paraphrase because too much of the original is left intact. In this area, instructors might step in and help the beginning researcher, for although these cases are not flagrant instances of plagiarism, such errors can mar an otherwise fine piece of research.

There is one safety net: Express clearly the name of your sources to let readers know the scope of your reading on the subject, as in this note in CMS footnote style:

> Commenting on the role that music has in our everyday lives, editor Marc Smirnoff makes this observation in <u>Oxford American:</u> "The music that human beings rely on is essential to them. We know which tunes to listen to when we need an all-important lift (or when the party does) or when we want to wallow in our sadness."[7]

Citations like the one above help establish your credibility because they make clear whom you have read and how your ideas blend with the source.

Scholarly documentation differs from field to field. The style of literary papers is different than that of scientific papers. In the social sci-

C H E C K L I S T

Documenting Your Sources

- Let a reader know when you begin borrowing from a source by introducing a quotation or paraphrase with the name of the authority.

- Enclose within quotation marks all quoted materials—keywords, phrases, sentences, paragraphs.

- Make certain that paraphrased material is rewritten in your own style and language. The simple rearrangement of sentence patterns is unacceptable.

- Provide specific in-text documentation for each borrowed item, but keep in mind that styles differ for MLA, APA, CSE, and CMS standards. These styles are explained in later chapters.

- Provide a bibliography entry on the Works Cited page for every source cited in the paper.

ences, a paraphrase does not require a page number. In the applied sciences, a number replaces the authority's name, the year, and even the page number. So you will find that standards shift considerably as you move from class to class and from discipline to discipline. The good writer learns to adapt to the changes in the academic standards. Accordingly, this book devotes separate chapters to Modern Language Association (MLA), American Psychological Association (APA), Council of Science Editors (CSE), and *Chicago Manual of Style* (CMS) styles.

Common Knowledge Exceptions

Common knowledge exceptions exist because you and your reader share some perspectives on a subject. For example, if you attend the University of Delaware, you need not cite the fact that Wilmington is the state's largest city, or that Dover is the capital city. Information of this sort requires *no* in-text citation because your local audience will be knowledgeable.

> The extended shoreline of Delaware provides one of the most extensive series of national wildlife refuges in the eastern United States. The state stretches from its northern border with Philadelphia to form a 100-mile border with Maryland

to its west and south. Its political center is Dover, in the center of the state, but its commercial center is Wilmington, a great industrial city situated on Delaware Bay just below Philadelphia.

However, a writer in another place and time might need to cite the source of this information. Most writers would probably want to document this next passage.

Early Indian tribes on the plains called themselves *Illiniwek* (which meant "strong men"), and French settlers pronounced the name *Illinois* (Angle 44).

Borrowing from a Source Correctly

The next examples in MLA style demonstrate the differences between the accurate use of a source and the dark shades of plagiarism. First is the original reference material; it is followed by several student versions, with discussions of their merits.

Original Material

Imagine your brain as a house filled with lights. Now imagine someone turning off the lights one by one. That's what Alzheimer's disease does. It turns off the lights so that the flow of ideas, emotions and memories from one room to the next slows and eventually ceases. And sadly—as anyone who has ever watched a parent, a sibling, a spouse succumb to the spreading darkness knows—there is no way to stop the lights from turning off, no way to switch them back on once they've grown dim. At least not yet.

But sooner than one might have dared hope, predicts Harvard University neurologist Dr. Dennis Selkoe, Alzheimer's disease will shed the veneer of invincibility that today makes it such a terrifying affliction. Medical practitioners, he believes, will shortly have on hand not one but several drugs capable of slowing—and perhaps even halting—the progression of the disease. Best of all, a better understanding of genetic and environmental risk factors will lead to much earlier diagnosis, so that patients will receive treatment long before their brains start to fade.

From J. Madeleine Nash, "The New Science of Alzheimer's," *Time* 17 July 2000: 51.

Student Version A (Needs Revision)

Alzheimer's disease is like having a brain that's similar to a house filled with lights, but somebody goes through the house and turns out the lights one by one until the brain, like the house, is dark.

This sentence sounds good, and the reader will probably think so also. However, the writer has borrowed the analogy and much of the wording from the original source, so it's not the student's work. In addition, the writer has provided no documentation whatsoever, nor has the writer named the authority. In truth, the writer implies to the reader that these sentences are an original creation when, actually, nothing belongs to the writer.

Student Version B (Needs Revision)

Alzheimer's is a terrifying disease, for both victim and relatives. However, sooner than we might expect, medical scientists will have available several drugs capable of slowing—and perhaps even halting—the progress of the disease. In addition, earlier diagnosis will mean patients can receive treatment before their brains start to go dark.

This version borrows keywords from the original without the use of quotation marks and without a citation. The next version provides a citation, but it too has errors.

Student Version C (Needs Minor Revision)

Alzheimer's is a terrifying disease, but help is on the way. Dr. Dennis Selkoe, a neurologist at Harvard University, predicts that medical practitioners will shortly have on hand several drugs that will slow or stop the progression of the disease (Nash 51).

This version is better. It provides a reference to Dr. Selkoe, who has been cited by Nash. But readers cannot know that the paraphrase contains far too much of Nash's language—words that should be enclosed within quotation marks. Also, the citation to Nash is ambiguous. The next version handles these matters in a better fashion.

Student Version D (Acceptable)

Alzheimer's is a terrifying disease, but help is on the way. In a recent report in *Time,* medical reporter Madeleine Nash cites Dr. Dennis Selkoe, a neurologist at Harvard University, who believes that "medical practitioners . . . will shortly have on hand not one but several drugs capable of slowing—and perhaps even halting—the progression of the disease" (Nash 51).

This version represents a satisfactory handling of the source material. The writer is acknowledged at the outset of the borrowing,

C H E C K L I S T

Required Instances for Citing a Source

Examples are in MLA style.

1. An original idea derived from a source, whether quoted or paraphrased.

   > Genetic engineering, by which a child's body shape and intellectual ability is predetermined, raised for one source "memories of Nazi attempts in eugenics" (Riddell 19).

2. Your summary of original ideas by a source.

   > Genetic engineering has been described as the rearrangement of the genetic structure in animals or in plants, which is a technique that takes a section of DNA and reattaches it to another section (Rosenthal 19–20).

3. Factual information that is not common knowledge within the context of the course.

   > Madigan has shown that genetic engineering has its risks: a nonpathogenic organism might be converted into a pathogenic one or an undesirable trait might develop as a result of a mistake (15).

4. Any exact wording copied from a source.

   > Woodward asserted that genetic engineering is "a high-stakes moral rumble that involves billions of dollars and affects the future" (68).

the neurologist is given credit for his ideas, and a key section is quoted. A correct page citation closes the material. Let's suppose, however, that the writer does not wish to quote directly at all. The following example shows a paraphrased version:

Student Version E (Acceptable)

Alzheimer's is a terrifying disease, but help is on the way. In a recent report in *Time,* medical reporter Madeleine Nash cites Dr. Dennis Selkoe, a neurologist at Harvard University, who believes that the scientific community is knocking on the door of a cure or maybe even a set of cures. The goal, according to Nash, is to halt the disease or at least slow its insidious stalking of some of our best and brightest, such as former President Ronald Reagan (Nash 51).

This version also represents a satisfactory handling of the source material. In this case, no direct quotation is employed, the author and the authority are acknowledged and credited, and the entire paragraph is paraphrased in the student's own language. *Note:* the reference to the former president is not mentioned in the original passage, but such usage is a prime example of common knowledge (see pages 59–60).

5e Seeking Permission to Publish Material on Your Web Site

You may wish to post your research papers on your personal Web site, if you have one. However, the moment you do so, you are *publishing* the work and putting it into the public domain. That act carries responsibilities. In particular, the *fair use* doctrine of the U.S. Code refers to the personal educational purposes of your usage. When you load borrowed images, text, music, or artwork onto the Internet, you are making that intellectual property available to everybody all over the world.

Short quotations, a few graphics, and a small quantity of illustrations to support your argument are examples of fair use. Permission is needed, however, if the amount you borrow is substantial. The borrowing cannot affect the market for the original work, and you cannot misrepresent it in any way. The courts are still refining the law. For example, would your use of three *Doonesbury* comic strips be substantial? Yes, if you reproduce them in full. Would it affect the market for the comic strip? Perhaps. Follow these guidelines:

- Seek permission to include copyrighted material you publish within your Web article. Most authors grant permission at no charge. The problem is tracking down the copyright holder.
- If you attempt to get permission and if your motive for using the material is *not for profit,* it's unlikely you will have any problem with the copyright owner. The owner would have to prove that your use of the image or text caused him or her financial harm.

- You may publish without permission works that are in the public domain, such a section of Hawthorne's *The Scarlet Letter* or a speech by the President from the White House. In general, creative works enter the public domain after about seventy-five years (the laws keep changing). Government papers are public domain.
- Document any and all sources you feature on your Web site.
- You may need permission to provide hypertext links to other sites. However, right now the Internet rules on access are being freely interpreted.
- Be prepared for other persons to visit your Web site and even borrow from it. Decide beforehand how you will handle requests for use of your work, especially if it includes your creative efforts in poetry, art, music, or graphic design.

HINT: For information on the Fair Use Laws, visit **http:// fairuse.stanford.edu/.**

6

Finding and Reading the Best Sources

Finding sources worthy of citation in your paper can be a challenge. This chapter cuts to the heart of the matter: How do you find the best, most appropriate sources? Should you read all or just part of a source? How do you respond to it? Also, in this age of electronic publications, you must constantly review and verify to your own satisfaction the words of your sources. It is wise to consider every article on the Internet as suspect unless you access it through your library's databases. See pages 44–45 for guidelines on judging the value of Internet articles.

6a Understanding the Assignment

A general search for sources on the Internet may serve your needs for writing a short paper, but the research paper requires you to compose from books, scholarly journals, and academic articles. Also, a specific academic discipline usually controls your research. For example, an assignment to examine the recreational programs at selected day care centers requires research in the literature of the social sciences found at your library's electronic catalogs rather than the Internet.

In addition, you need a mix of primary and secondary sources. *Primary sources* include novels, speeches, eyewitness accounts, interviews, letters, autobiographies, observation during field research, and the written results of empirical research. You should feel free to quote often from a primary source that has direct relevance to your discussion. For example, if you present a poem by Dylan Thomas, you should quote the poem. *Secondary sources* are writings about the primary sources, about an author, or about somebody's accomplishments. Secondary sources include a report on a presidential speech, a review of new scientific findings, analysis of a poem, or a biography of a notable person. These evaluations, analyses, and interpretations provide ways of looking at original, primary sources. Here's a guide to sources for the major disciplines.

Guide to Academic Sources

Humanities

Primary sources in literature and the fine arts are novels, poems, and plays as well as films, paintings, music, and sculpture. Your task is to examine, interpret, and evaluate these original works. Researchers in history must look at speeches, documents written by historic figures, and some government documents.

Secondary sources in the humanities are evaluations in journal articles and books, critical reviews, biographies, and history books.

Field research in the humanities comprises interviews with an artist or government official, letters, e-mail surveys, online discussion groups, and the archival study of manuscripts.

Social Sciences

Primary sources in education, political science, psychology, and other fields include speeches, writings by presidents and others, documents recorded in the *Congressional Record,* reports and statistics of government agencies and departments, and papers at your state's archival library.

Field research is most important in the social sciences and consists of case studies, findings from surveys and questionnaires, tests and test data, interviews, and observation. In business reports, field research consists of market testing, drawings and designs, industrial research, letters, and interviews.

Secondary sources include books and articles on social, political, and psychological issues, analyses and evaluations in journal articles, discussions of the business world in newspapers, magazines, and journals, and—in general—anything written about key personalities, events, products, and primary documents.

Sciences

Primary sources in the sciences consist of the words and theories of scientists discussing natural phenomena or offering their views on scientific issues, such as the words of Charles Darwin or Stephen Hawking. At the same time, journal articles that report on empirical research are considered primary material because they are original in their testing of a hypothesis.

Secondary sources in the sciences are not abundant. They appear generally as review articles that discuss testing and experiments by several scientists—for example, the review of four or five articles on gene mutation.

Field research and laboratory testing are crucial to the sciences and provide the results of experiments, discoveries, tests, and observations.

6b Identifying the Best Source Materials

Let's look at an inverted pyramid that shows you a progression from excellent sources to less reliable ones. The chart does not ask you to ignore or dismiss items at the bottom, such as magazines and e-mail discussion groups, but it lets you know when to feel confident and when to be on guard about the validity of the source.

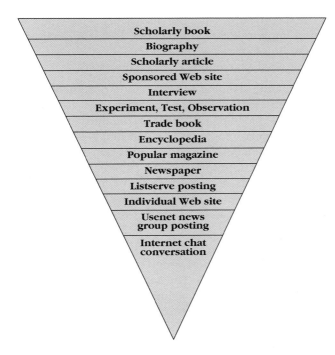

Scholarly book
Biography
Scholarly article
Sponsored Web site
Interview
Experiment, Test, Observation
Trade book
Encyclopedia
Popular magazine
Newspaper
Listserve posting
Individual Web site
Usenet news group posting
Internet chat conversation

Scholarly Book

Scholarly books, including textbooks, treat academic topics with in-depth discussions and careful documentation of the evidence. A college library is a repository for scholarly books—technical and scientific works, doctoral dissertations, publications of the university presses, and many textbooks. Scholarly books are subjected to careful review before publication, and they are published because they give the very best treatment of a subject. However, in the sciences, books grow out of date quickly, so depend on monthly journals to keep your research current.

Biography

The library's electronic catalog can help you find an appropriate biography from among the thousands available; representative databases include *Contemporary Authors* and *Dictionary of American Negro Biography.* You can also learn about a notable person on the Internet by searching for the name of the person and carefully scanning the sites that are returned. Notable persons are likely to have a Web site devoted to them. A *critical biography* is a book devoted not only to the life of the subject but also to his or her life's work; an excellent example is Richard Ellmann's *Oscar Wilde,* a critical study of Wilde's writings as well as his life.

You may need a biography for several reasons:

- To verify the standing and reputation of somebody you want to paraphrase or quote in your paper.
- To provide biographical details in your introduction. For example, the primary topic may be Carl Jung's psychological theories of the unconscious, but information about Jung's career might also be appropriate in the paper.
- To discuss a creative writer's life in relation to his or her work—that is, details of Joyce Carol Oates's personal life may illuminate your reading of her stories and novels.

Scholarly Article

Scholarly articles are best found through one of the library's databases (see pages 17–22). The academic database takes you to journal articles or articles at academically sponsored Web sites. You can feel confident about the authenticity of journal articles because the authors write for academic honor, they document all sources, and they publish through university presses and academic organizations. Thus, a journal article about child abuse found in *Journal of Marriage and the Family* or found through the PsyINFO database may be considered reliable. Nevertheless, some popular magazines are noted for their quality, such as *Atlantic Monthly, Scientific Review,* and *Discover.* The major newspapers—*New York Times, Atlanta Constitution,* and *Wall Street Journal*—often hire the best writers and columnists, so valuable articles can be found in both printed and online newspapers.

Sponsored Web Site

The Internet supplies both excellent and dubious information. You must be careful when evaluating Web materials. Chapter 3 explores research on the Web. In addition to the checklist on pages 44–45, "Evaluating Internet Sources," you should also ask yourself a few questions about any Web site information:

- Is it appropriate to my work?
- Does it reveal a serious and scholarly emphasis?
- Is it sponsored by a professional institution or organization?

Interview

Interviews with knowledgeable people provide excellent information for a research paper. Whether conducted in person, by telephone, or by e-mail, the interview brings a personal, expert perspective to your work. The key element, of course, is the experience of the person. For full details about conducting an interview, see page 48. For an example of an interview used in a research paper, see pages 161–62.

Experiment, Test, or Observation

Gathering your own data for research is a staple in many fields, especially the sciences. An experiment brings primary evidence into your paper as you explain your hypothesis, give the test results, and discuss the implications of your findings. For a full discussion on conducting scientific investigation, with guidelines and details on format, see pages 52–54.

Trade Book

How to Launch a Small Business and *Landscaping with Rocks* are typical titles of nonfiction trade books found in bookstores rather than college libraries (although public libraries often have trade book holdings). Designed for commercial consumption, trade books seldom treat a scholarly subject in depth. Unlike scholarly books and textbooks, manuscripts for trade books do not go through the rigors of peer review. For example, if your topic is dieting, with a focus on fad diets, you will find plenty of diet books at the local bookstore and numerous articles on commercial Web sites. However, serious discussions backed by careful research are found in the journals or at sponsored Web sites.

Encyclopedia

An encyclopedia, by design, contains brief surveys of every well-known person, event, place, and accomplishment. It can support your preliminary investigation for a topic, but most instructors prefer that you go beyond encyclopedias to cite from scholarly books and journal articles. However, specialized encyclopedias (see pages 23–24) often have in-depth articles by noted scholars.

Popular Magazine

Like a trade book, a magazine article seldom offers in-depth information and does not face the critical review of a panel of experts. Thus, you must exercise caution when using it as a source. In general, college libraries house the better magazines—those that have merit in the quality of writing—so depend on the library's list of academic databases. For example, if your paper concerns sports medicine, citing an article from the *Atlantic Monthly* or *Scientific Review* will gain you far higher marks than one from *Sports Illustrated, Sport,* or *NBA Basketball.*

Newspaper

Newspaper reporters write under the pressure of deadlines. They do not have as much time to do careful research as do writers of journal articles. On occasion, a newspaper assigns reporters to a series of articles on a complex topic, and such in-depth analyses have merit. As noted above, the major newspapers—*New York Times, Atlanta Constitution,* and *Wall Street Journal*—often hire highly qualified writers and columnists, so valuable articles can be found in both the printed and online versions of these papers. You must remember, however, that newspaper articles, like those in magazines and on the Internet, must receive cautionary and critical evaluation.

E-mail Discussion Group

E-mail information via a forum established by the instructor for an course deserves consideration when it focuses on academic issues such as British Romantic literature or, more specifically, Shelley's poetry. In some cases, they originate for students in an online course, providing a venue for sharing ideas. However, rather than search for quotable material from e-mail forums, use them as a sounding board to generate ideas and test them with other participants.

Individual Web Site

Anyone can set up a Web site regardless of his or her credentials. You cannot avoid unreliable sites because they pop up on search engines, but you can approach them with caution. For example, a student investigating the topic *fad diets* searched the Web but found mostly home pages that described personal battles with weight loss or commercial sites that were blatant in their attempts to sell. Caution is vital.

Internet Chat Conversations

Real-time Internet conversations have almost no value for academic research and are not legitimate sources for your paper. Seldom do you know the participants beyond their usernames, and the conversations seldom focus on scholarly issues.

 Evaluating a Source

Confronted by several books and articles, many writers have trouble determining the value of material and the contribution it can make to the research paper. To save time, you must be selective in your reading. To serve your reader, you must cite carefully selected material that is pertinent to the argument. Avoid dumping huge blocks of quotation into the paper because the paper will lack your style and tone of voice. You must be concerned about the relevance, authority, accuracy, and currency of all sources you cite in your paper.

Relevance

To determine how well an article or book fits the demands of your research, skim it. For a periodical or Internet article, examine the title, the abstract or introduction, and both the opening and closing paragraphs.

Authority

To test the authority of a source, examine the credentials of the author (usually found in a brief biographical profile or note of professional affiliation) and the sponsoring institution—usually the publisher of a journal, such as the American Sociological Association, or the sponsor of a Web site, such as **http://www.ucla.edu**. Look at the bibliography at the end of the article, for it signals the scholarly nature of the work and also points you toward other material on the subject. Study the home page of an Internet article, if there is one. Prefer sites sponsored by universities and professional organizations. Note hypertext links to other sites whose quality may be determined by the domain tags, such as .edu, .org, and .gov. Be wary of .com sites.

Note: The definitive edition of a work is the most reliable version of a play, novel, or collection of poems; it is definitive because it is the one the author supervised through the press. The way an author wanted the work presented can be found only in a definitive edition. Thus, electronic versions usually do not display the original author's page and type design, unless they are photocopies of the original, as at the JSTOR site (see page 20).

Accuracy

In the sciences, scholars talk about the verification of an article, which means they can, if necessary, replicate the research and the findings. A scientific report must carefully detail the design of the work, the methods, subjects, and procedures. A lab experiment, for example, should repeat previous findings to demonstrate accuracy. The writer should reveal the details of a control group, an experimental group, and the testing procedures. Any scientific report that does not establish research methods should not be cited.

Currency

Use recent sources for research in the sciences and social sciences. A psychology book may look valuable, but if its copyright date is 1955 the content has probably been replaced by recent research and current developments. When reading a source, be certain at least one date is listed. Electronic publications sometimes show the site has been updated or refreshed, but the article itself may carry an older date. On the Internet, check the date of print publication; it may be different than that of the Web publication. As a general rule, use the most recent date for an article on the Internet, which means you could list as many as three dates—the year of the print publication, the most recent year of the Internet publication, and the date you accessed the material.

7

Organizing Ideas and Setting Goals

Initially, research is haphazard, and your workspace will be cluttered with bits of information on notes and photocopied sheets. After investigating and gathering sufficient sources for your project, you must organize the information to serve specific needs. The structure of your project will become clear only when you organize your research materials into a proposal, a list of ideas, a set of questions, or a rough outline. In most cases, the design of your study should match an appropriate organizational model, sometimes called a *paradigm*, which means "an example that serves as a pattern or model." The organizational models in this chapter will help you organize your notes, photocopies, and downloaded files. Research assignments demand different kinds of papers in a variety of formats. By following an academic model, you can be assured the design of your research project will meet the demands of the assignment.

7a Using the Correct Academic Model (Paradigm)

A traditional outline, because it is content-specific, is useful for one paper only, while an academic pattern, like those shown below, governs all papers within a certain design. For example, a general, all-purpose model gives a plan for almost any research topic.

A General, All-Purpose Model

If you are uncertain about your assignment, start with this basic model and expand it with your own material to develop a detailed outline. Readers, including your instructor, are accustomed to this sequence for research papers. It offers plenty of leeway.

- Identify the subject in the *introduction*. Explain the problem, provide background information, and give a clear thesis statement.

- Analyze the subject in the *body* of the paper. You can compare, analyze, give evidence, trace historical events, and handle other matters.
- Discuss your findings in the *conclusion*. You can challenge an assumption, interpret the findings, provide solutions, or reaffirm your thesis.

The specific design of any model is based on the nature of the assignment and the discipline for which you are writing. Each of the following forms is explained below.

Academic Pattern for the Interpretation of Literature and Other Creative Works

If you plan to interpret a musical, artistic, or literary work, such as an opera, a group of paintings, or a novel, adjust this model to your subject and purpose and build it, with your factual data, into a working outline.

Introduction
>Identify the work.
>Give a brief summary in one sentence.
>Provide background information that relates to the thesis.
>Offer biographical facts about the artist that relate to the specific issues.
>Quote and paraphrase authorities to establish the scholarly traditions.
>Write a thesis sentence that establishes your particular views of the literary work.

Body
>Provide evaluative analysis divided by imagery, theme, design, use of color, character development, structure, symbolism, narration, language, musical themes, and so forth.

Conclusion
>Focus on the artist, not just the elements of analysis as explained in the body.
>Explore the contributions of the artist in accordance with your thesis sentence.

Academic Pattern for the Analysis of History

If you are writing a history or political science paper that analyzes events and their causes and consequences, your paper should conform, in general, to the following plan. Flesh it out with the notes in your research journal to make it a working outline for drafting your paper.

Introduction
  Identify the event.
  Provide the background leading up to the event.
  Offer quotations and paraphrases from experts.
  Give the thesis sentence.
Body
  Analyze the background leading up to the event.
  Trace events from one historic episode to another.
  Offer a chronological sequence that explains how one event
    relates directly to the next.
  Cite authorities who have also investigated this event.
Conclusion
  Reaffirm your thesis.
  Discuss the consequences of this event.

Academic Pattern for Advancing Philosophical and Religious Ideas

If the assignment is to defend or analyze a topic from the history of ideas, use this next design, adjusting it as necessary. Make it your working outline by writing sentences and even paragraphs for each item in the model.

Introduction
  Establish the idea or question.
  Trace its history.
  Discuss its significance.
  Introduce experts who have addressed the idea.
  Provide a thesis sentence that presents your approach to the
    issue(s)—from a fresh perspective, if at all possible.
Body
  Evaluate the issues surrounding the concept.
  Develop a past-to-present examination of theories.
  Compare and analyze the details and minor issues.
  Cite experts who have addressed this idea.
Conclusion
  Advance and defend your thesis as it grows out of evidence
    about the idea.
  Close with an effective quotation from a noted person.

Academic Pattern for the Review of a Performance

If the assignment is to review a musical, artistic, or literary performance, such as an opera, a set of paintings, a reading, a drama, or theatrical performance, adjust this paradigm to your subject and purpose. *Note:* The review differs from the interpretation (see page 74) by its focus on evaluation rather than analysis.

Introduction
  Identify the work.
  Give a brief summary in one sentence.
  Provide background information or history of the work.
  Offer biographical facts about the artist that relate to the specific issues.
  Quote and paraphrase authorities to establish the scholarly traditions that relate to this work and the performance.
  Write a thesis sentence that establishes your judgment of the performance.
Body
  Offer an evaluation based on a predetermined set of criteria. Judge a drama by its staging and acting, music by its quality of voice and instruments, art by its design, literature by its themes, and so forth.
Conclusion
  Focus on the performance, the performers, and the artist.
  Offer a judgment based on the criteria given in the body.

Academic Pattern for Advancing Your Ideas and Theories

If you want to advance a social or legal theory in your paper, use this design, adjusting it to eliminate unnecessary items and adding new elements as appropriate. Build this model into a working outline by assigning your notes, photocopies, and downloaded files to a specific line of the model.

Introduction
  Establish the theory, problem, or question.
  Discuss its significance.
  Provide the necessary background information.
  Introduce experts who have addressed the problem.
  Provide a thesis sentence that relates the problem to a fresh perspective.
Body
  Evaluate the issues involved in the problem.
  Develop a chronological examination.
  Compare and analyze the details and minor issues.
  Cite experts who have addressed the same problem.
Conclusion
  Advance and defend your theory.

Discuss the implications of your findings.

Offer directives or a plan of action.

Suggest additional research that might be appropriate.

Academic Pattern for Argument and Persuasion Papers

If you write persuasively or argue from a set position, your paper should conform, in general, to this paradigm. Select the elements that fit your design, begin to elaborate on them, and gradually build a frame for your paper.

Introduction
> Establish clearly the problem or controversy that your paper will examine.
>
> Summarize the issues.
>
> Define key terminology.
>
> Make concessions on some points of the argument.
>
> Use quotations and paraphrases to explore the controversy.
>
> Provide background information.
>
> Write a thesis to establish your position.

Body
> Develop arguments to defend one side of the subject.
>
> Analyze the issues, both pro and con.
>
> Give evidence from the sources, including quotations from the scholarship as appropriate.

Conclusion
> Expand your thesis into a conclusion to demonstrate that your position was formulated logically through careful analysis and discussion of the issues.

Academic Model for a Comparative Study

A comparative study requires that you examine two schools of thought, two issues, two works, or the positions taken by two persons. It explores similarities and differences, generally using one of three arrangements for the body of the paper. As you embellish the model you will gradually build your working outline.

Introduction
> Establish A.
>
> Establish B.
>
> Briefly compare the two.
>
> Introduce the central issues.
>
> Cite source materials on the subjects.
>
> Present your thesis.

Body (choose one)

Examine A.	Compare A and B.	Issue 1: Discuss A and B.
Examine B.	Contrast A and B.	Issue 2: Discuss A and B.
Compare and contrast A and B.	Discuss the central issues.	Issue 3: Discuss A and B.

Conclusion

Discuss the significant issues.

Rank one of the subjects over the other, or rate the respective genius of each.

Academic Pattern for a Laboratory Investigation or Field Report

This model has little flexibility. Instructors will expect your report to remain tightly focused on each of these items.

Introduction

Provide the title, the experiment number, and the date.

Describe the experiment.

List any literature consulted.

Objectively describe what you hope to accomplish.

Method

Explain the procedures used to reproduce the experiment.

Explain the design of the test.

Identify any tools or apparatus used.

Identify any variables that affected your research (weather conditions, temperatures, and so on).

Results

Give your findings, including statistical data.

Discussion

Provide your interpretation of the data.

Discuss implications to be drawn from the research.

Comment on what you learned by the experiment (optional).

Academic Pattern for Scientific Analysis

In this situation, you are working with the literature on a scientific issue, so you have more flexibility than with a report on a lab experiment.

Introduction

Identify the scientific issue or problem and state your hypothesis.

Explore the history of the topic.

Cite the literature that pertains to the topic.

Explain the purpose of the examination and its possible implications.

Body

Classify the issues.

Analyze, define, and compare each aspect of the topic.

Offer cause-effect explanations.

Make a detailed inquiry into all relevant issues.

Conclusion

Explain the current findings of scientific studies related to your topic.

Advance your reasons for continued research.

Suggest possible findings.

Discuss the implications of your analysis.

Academic Pattern for a Report of Empirical Research

This pattern is similar to the one for a laboratory investigation, so follow it closely to fill all the required items.

Introduction

Present the point of your study.

State the hypothesis and how it relates to the problem.

Provide the theoretical implications.

Explain the manner in which your study relates to previously published work.

Method

Describe the subject (what was tested, who participated— whether human or animal—and where the field work was accomplished).

Describe your equipment and how you used it.

Summarize the procedure and the execution of each stage of your work.

Results

Summarize the data you collected.

Provide statistical treatment of your findings with tables, graphs, and charts.

Include findings that conflict with your hypothesis.

Discussion

Discuss the implications of your work.

Evaluate the data and its relevance to the hypothesis.

Interpret the findings as necessary.

Discuss the implications of the findings.

Qualify the results and limit them to your specific study.

Make inferences from the results.

Suggest areas worthy of additional research.

7b Using Your Thesis to Control the Outline

After you have selected an academic pattern appropriate to your assignment, you should use your thesis sentence (or hypothesis) to set the tone and direction of your paper. Notice below how variations in the thesis can affect the arrangement of the paper.

Argument

THESIS: Misunderstandings about organ donation distort reality and set serious limits on the availability of organs to persons who need an eye, a liver, or a healthy heart.

Argument 1. Many myths mislead people into believing that donation is unethical.

Argument 2. Some fear that as a patient they might be put down early.

Argument 3. Religious views sometimes get in the way of donation.

This preliminary outline gives this writer three categories for an analysis of the issues.

Cause and Effect

THESIS: Television can have positive effects on a child's language development.

Consequence 1. Television introduces new words.

Consequence 2. Television reinforces word usage and proper syntax.

Consequence 3. Literary classics come alive on television.

Consequence 4. Television exposes children to the subtle rhythms and musical effects of accomplished speakers.

Notice that the thesis on television's educational values points the way to four issues worthy of investigation.

Evaluation

THESIS: The architectural drawing for the university's new student center is not friendly to people who are handicapped.

Evaluation 1.	The common areas seem cramped and narrow, with few open areas in which students can cluster.
Evaluation 2.	Steps and stairs seem all too common in the design.
Evaluation 3.	Only one elevator appears in the plans when three would be fair and equitable.
Evaluation 4.	Only the first-floor rest rooms offer universal access.
Evaluation 5.	The parking spaces designated for people with physical handicaps are located at an entrance with steps, not a ramp.

This outline evolves from a thesis sentence that invites evaluation of an architectural plan.

Comparison

THESIS: Discipline often involves punishment, but child abuse adds another element: the gratification of the adult.

Comparison 1.	A spanking has the interest of the child at heart, but a beating or a caning has no redeeming value.
Comparison 2.	Time-outs remind the child that relationships are important and to be cherished, but lockouts in a closet only promote hysteria and fear.
Comparison 3.	The parent's ego and selfish interests often take precedence over the welfare of the child or children.

This thesis sentence motivates a pattern of comparison by which to judge the relative differences between punishment of a child and child abuse.

7c   Writing an Outline

Not all papers require a complete, formal outline, nor do all researchers need one. A short research paper can be created from keywords, a list of issues, a rough outline, and a first draft. However, an outline sometimes is important, for it fleshes out the academic pattern you have selected (see section 7a) by classifying the issues of your study into clear, logical categories with main headings and one or more levels of subheadings.

A formal outline is not rigid and inflexible; you may, and should, modify it while writing and revising. In every case, treat an outline or organizational chart as a tool. Like an architect's blueprint, it should contribute to, not inhibit, the construction of a finished product. You may wish to experiment with the Outline feature of your software, which allows you to view the paper at various levels of detail and to highlight and drop the essay into a different organization.

Topic Outline

Build a topic outline of balanced phrases. You can use noun phrases ("the rods of the retina"), gerund phrases ("sensing dim light with retina rods"), or infinitive phrases ("to sense dim light with retina rods"). No matter which grammatical format you choose, follow it consistently throughout the outline. One student used noun phrases to outline her scientific analysis:

I. Diabetes defined
   A. A disease without control
      1. A disorder of the metabolism
      2. The search for a cure
   B. Types of diabetes
      1. Type 1, juvenile diabetes
      2. Type 2, adult onset diabetes
II. Health complications
   A. The problem of hyperglycemia
      1. Signs and symptoms of the problem
      2. Lack of insulin
   B. The conflict of the kidneys and the liver
      1. Effects of ketoacidosis
      2. Effects of arteriosclerosis
III. Proper care and control
   A. Blood sugar monitoring
      1. Daily monitoring at home
      2. Hemoglobin test at a laboratory
   B. Medication for diabetes
      1. Insulin injections
      2. Hypoglycemia agents

     C. Exercise programs
        1. Walking
        2. Swimming
        3. Aerobic workouts
     D. Diet and meal planning
        1. Exchange plan
        2. Carbohydrate counting
IV. Conclusion: Balance of all the factors

Sentence Outline

    Instead of an outline with phrases, you may use full sentences for each heading and subheading. Using sentences has two advantages over the topic outline: (1) Many entries in a sentence outline can serve as topic sentences for paragraphs, thereby accelerating the writing process, and (2) The subject-verb pattern establishes the logical direction of your thinking (for example, the phrase *Vocabulary development* becomes *Television viewing can improve a child's vocabulary*). Note below a brief portion of one student's sentence outline.

    I. Organ and tissue donation is the gift of life.
     A. Organs that can be successfully transplanted include the heart, lungs, liver, kidneys, and pancreas.
     B. Tissues that can be transplanted successfully include bone, corneas, skin, heart valves, veins, cartilage, and other connective tissues.
     C. The process of becoming a donor is easy.
     D. Many people receive organ and tissue transplants each year, but still many people die because they did not receive the needed transplant.

8

Writing
Effective Notes

Notetaking is the heart of research. If you write notes of high quality, they may need only minor editing to fit the appropriate places in your first draft. Prepare yourself to write different types of notes—quotations for well-phrased passages by authorities but also paraphrased or summarized notes to maintain your voice. This chapter explains the following types of notes:

- *Personal notes* that express your own ideas or record field research.
- *Quotation notes* that preserve the distinguished syntax of an authority.
- *Paraphrase notes* that interpret and restate what the authority has said.
- *Summary notes* that capture in capsule form a writer's ideas.
- *Field notes* that record interviews, tabulate questionnaires, and maintain records of laboratory experiments and other types of field research.

Honoring the Conventions of Research Style

Your notetaking will be more effective from the start if you practice the conventions of style for citing a source within your text, as advocated by MLA, APA, CSE, or CMS and as shown briefly below (see pages 104–06 for a full explanation of the differences in MLA, APA, CMS, and CSE).

MLA: Lawrence Smith states, "The suicidal teen causes severe damage to the psychological condition of peers" (34).

APA: Smith (1997) stated, "The suicidal teen causes severe damage to the psychological condition of peers" (p. 34).

CMS footnote: Lawrence Smith explains, "The suicidal teen causes severe damage to the psychological condition of peers."[3]

C H E C K L I S T

Writing Effective Notes

1. Write each note in a separate, labeled file within one folder, although you can keep several notes in one computer file if each is labeled clearly. Remember, downloaded files from Internet databases must also be labeled clearly.

2. Accompany each file with the name, year, and page of the source to prepare for in-text citations.

3. Label each file (for example, *objectivity on television).*

4. Write a full note in well-developed sentences to speed the writing of your first draft.

5. Keep everything (photocopy, scribbled note) in order to authenticate dates, page numbers, and full names.

6. Label your personal notes with *my idea* or *personal note* to distinguish them from the sources.

CSE number: Smith (4) said, "The suicidal teen causes severe damage to the psychological condition of peers."

The MLA style is the default style displayed throughout this chapter.

8a   Writing Personal Notes

The content of a research paper is an expression of your own ideas as supported by the scholarly evidence. It is not a collection of ideas transmitted by experts in books and articles. Readers are primarily interested in *your* thesis sentence, *your* topic sentences, and *your* personal view of the issues. Therefore, during your research, record your thoughts on the issues by writing plenty of personal notes in your research journal and computer files. Personal notes are essential because they allow you to record your discoveries, reflect on the findings, make connections, and identify the prevailing views and patterns of thought. Remember two standards: (1) The idea written into the file is yours, and (2) the file is labeled with *my idea, mine, personal thought* to distinguish it from information borrowed from a source. Here's an example:

Personal thought

For me, organ donation might be a gift of life, so I have signed my donor card. At least a part of me will continue to live if an accident claims my life. My boyfriend says I'm gruesome, but I consider it practical. Besides, he might be the one who benefits, and then what will he say?

8b Writing Direct Quotation Notes

Quotation notes are essential because they allow you to capture the authoritative voices of the experts on the topic, feature well-phrased statements, offer conflicting points of view, and share the literature on the topic with your readers. Follow these basic conventions.

1. Select material that is important and well-phrased, not something trivial or something that is common knowledge. Not "John F. Kennedy was a Democrat from Massachusetts" (Rupert 233) but this:

   "John F. Kennedy's Peace Corps left a legacy of lasting compassion for the downtrodden"(Rupert 233).

2. Use quotation marks around the quoted material in your notes, working draft, and final manuscript. Do not copy or download the words of a source into your paper in such a way that readers will think *you* wrote the material.

3. Use the exact words of the source.

4. Provide an appropriate in-text citation, as in this note:

   Griffiths, Kilman, and Frost suggest that the killing of architect Stanford White in 1904 was "the beginning of the most bitterly savage century known to mankind" (113). Murder, wars, and human atrocities were the "sad vestiges" of an era that had great promise.

5. The parenthetical citation goes *outside* the final quotation mark but *inside* the period for quotations within your sentence. Block quotations require a different setup (see page 88).

6. Quote key sentences and short passages, not entire paragraphs. Find the essential statement and feature it; do not force your reader to read a long quoted passage that has only one statement relevant to your point. Make the essential idea a part of your sentence, as shown here:

   Many Americans, trying to mend their past eating habits, adopt functional foods as an essential step toward a more

health-conscious future. Balthrop says this group of
believers spends "an estimated $29 billion a year" on
functional foods (6).

7. Quote from both primary sources (the original words of a writer
or speaker) and secondary sources (comments after the fact about
original works). The two types are discussed immediately below.

Quoting the Primary Sources

Quote from primary sources for four reasons:

- To draw on the wisdom of the original author
- To let readers hear the precise words of the author
- To copy exact lines of poetry and drama
- To reproduce graphs, charts, and statistical data

Cite poetry, fiction, drama, letters, and interviews. In other cases,
you may want to quote liberally from a presidential speech, cite the
words of a business executive, or reproduce original data.

Quoting the Secondary Sources

Quote from secondary sources for three reasons:

- To display excellence in ideas and expression by experts on
the topic
- To explain complex material
- To set up a statement of your own, especially if it spins off,
adds to, or takes exception to the source as quoted

The overuse of direct quotation from secondary sources indicates either (1) that you did not have a clear focus and copied ver-
batim just about everything related to the subject, or (2) that you had
inadequate evidence and used numerous quotations as padding.
Therefore, limit quotations from secondary sources by using only a
phrase or a sentence:

Reginald Herman says the geographical changes in Russia
require "intensive political analysis" (15).

If you quote an entire sentence, make the quotation a direct
object that tells *what* the authority says.

In response to the changes in Russia, one critic notes, "The
American government must exercise caution and conduct
intensive political analysis" (15).

8c Writing Paraphrased Notes

A paraphrase requires you to restate in your own words the thought, meaning, and attitude of someone else. Your interpretation acts as a bridge between the source and the reader as you capture the wisdom of the source in approximately the same number of words. Use paraphrase to maintain your voice or style in the paper, to avoid an endless string of direct quotations, and to interpret the source as you rewrite it. Keep in mind these five rules for paraphrasing a source:

1. Rewrite the original in about the same number of words.
2. Provide an in-text citation to the source (in MLA style, the author and page number).
3. Retain exceptional words and phrases from the original by enclosing them in quotation marks.
4. Preserve the tone of the original by suggesting moods of satire, anger, humor, doubt, and so on. Show the author's attitude with appropriate verbs: "Edward Zigler condemns . . . defends . . . argues . . . explains . . . observes . . . defines."
5. Put the original aside while paraphrasing to avoid copying word for word. Compare the finished paraphrase with the original source to be certain that the paraphrase truly rewrites the original and that it uses quotation marks with any phrasing or key words retained from the original.

HINT: When instructors see an in-text citation but no quotation marks, they will assume that you are paraphrasing, not quoting. Be sure their assumption is correct.

Here are examples that show the differences between a quotation note and a paraphrased one:

Quotation:

Hein explains heredity in this way: "Except for identical twins, each person's heredity is unique" (294).

Paraphrase:

One source explains that heredity is special and distinct for each of us, unless a person is one of identical twins (Hein 294).

Quotation (block indent of four lines or more):

Hein explains the phenomenon in this way:

> Since only half of each parent's chromosomes are transmitted to a child and since this half

represents a chance selection of those the child
could inherit, only twins that develop from a
single fertilized egg that splits in two have
identical chromosomes. (294)

Paraphrase:

Hein specifies that twins have identical chromosomes
because they grow from one egg that divides after it has been
fertilized. He affirms that most brothers and sisters differ
because of the "chance selection" of chromosomes
transmitted by each parent (294).

As shown in the example immediately above, place any key
wording of the source within quotation marks.

8d | Writing Summary Notes

A summary of a source serves a specific purpose, so it deserves
a polished style for transfer into the paper. It requires you to capture
in just a few words the ideas of an entire paragraph, section, or chapter. Store it in your folder with its own file name. It may be a rough
sketch of the source or a polished note. Use it for these reasons:

- To review an article or book
- To annotate a bibliography entry
- To provide a plot summary
- To create an abstract

Success with the summary requires the following:

1. Condense the original content with precision and directness.
   Reduce a long paragraph to a sentence, tighten an article into a
   brief paragraph, and summarize a book in a page.
2. Preserve the tone of the original. If the original is serious, suggest that tone in the summary. In the same way, retain moods of
   doubt, skepticism, optimism, and so forth.
3. Write the summary in your own language; however, retain exceptional phrases from the original, enclosing them in quotation marks.
4. Provide documentation.

Use the Summary to Review Briefly an Article or Book

Note this example, which reviews two entire articles:

Alec Twobears has two closely related articles on this subject,
and both, one in 2001 and another in 2002, are about the

failure of the United States to follow through with the treaties it signed with the Indian nations of North America. He opens both with "No treaty is a good treaty!" He signals clearly the absence of trust by native Americans toward the government in Washington, DC.

To see more summaries of this type, presented in a review of the literature, see pages 95–100.

Use the Summary to Write an Annotated Bibliography

An annotation offers a brief explanation or critical commentary on an article or book. Thus, an annotated bibliography is one in which each source is followed immediately by the annotation, as shown here in MLA style.

"Top Ten Myths about Donation and Transplantation."
TransWeb Webcast, 2002. 10 Oct. 2003 <http://www.transweb.org/news/zhtm>. This site dispels the many myths surrounding organ donation, showing that selling organs is illegal, that matching donor and recipient is highly complicated, and secret back room operations are almost impossible.

See pages 92–94 to view more annotated bibliography entries.

Use the Summary in a Plot Summary Note

In just a few sentences, a summary can describe a novel, short story, drama, or similar literary work, as shown by this next note:

Great Expectations by Dickens describes young Pip, who inherits money and can live the life of a gentleman. But he discovers that his "great expectations" have come from a criminal. With that knowledge his attitude changes from one of vanity to one of compassion.

Use the Summary to Create an Abstract

An abstract is a brief description that appears at the beginning of an article to summarize the contents. Usually, it is written by the article's author, and it helps readers make decisions about reading the entire article. You can find entire volumes devoted to abstracts, such as *Psychological Abstracts* and *Abstracts of English Studies.* An abstract is required for most papers in the social and natural sciences. Here's a sample from one student's paper:

Abstract

Functional foods, products that provide benefits beyond basic nutrition, are adding billions to the nation's economy each year. Functional foods are suspected to be a form of preventive medicine. Consumers hope that functional foods can calm some of their medical anxieties, while researchers believe that functional foods may lower health care costs. The paper identifies several functional foods, locates the components that make them work, and explains the role that each plays on the body.

See pages 159 and 184 for additional examples of abstracts.

8e   Writing Notes from Field Research

For some research projects, you will be expected to conduct field research. This work may require different kinds of notes kept on charts, cards, notepads, laboratory notebooks, a research journal, or the computer. Interviews require careful notetaking during the session and dutiful transcription of those notes to your draft. A tape recorder can serve as a backup to your notetaking. A questionnaire produces valuable data for developing notes and graphs and charts for your research paper.

The procedures and findings of experiments, tests, and measurements serve as your notes for the Method and Results sections of the report. Here is an example of one student's laboratory notebook—a passage he might transfer to the Procedures section of his paper:

First, 25.0 ml of a vinegar sample was delivered to a 50-ml volumetric flask, with a 25-ml pipet, and diluted to the mark with distilled water. It was mixed thoroughly and 50.00-ml aliquot were emptied into three 250-ml conical flasks, with a 25-ml pipet, 50 ml of distilled water, and two drops of phenolphthalein were added to each of the flasks. The samples were then titrated with a .345 M NaOH solution until the first permanent pink color.

8f Using Your Notes to Write an Annotated Bibliography

Writing an annotated bibliography may look like busywork, but it helps you evaluate the strength and nature of your sources. The annotated bibliography that follows is written in MLA style. An *annotation* is a summary of the contents of a book or article. A *bibliography* is a list of sources on a selected topic. Thus, an annotated bibliography does two important things: (1) it lists bibliographic data for a selection of sources, and (2) it summarizes the contents of each book or article.

The annotated bibliography that follows summarizes a few sources on the issue of tanning, tanning beds, lotions, and the dangers of skin cancer.

Levenson 1

Norman Levenson
Professor Davidson
English 1020
24 July 2003

Annotated Bibliography

Brown, Edwin W. "Tanning Beds and the 'Safe Tan'
Myth." <u>Medical Update</u> 21 (1998): 6. Brown makes
the point that there is "no such thing as a 'safe' or
'healthy' tan. " He explains that tanning is the skin's
reaction to radiation damage, and "tanned skin is
damaged skin." He cautions that tans from tanning
beds are no different than those produced by the
sun. Like others, he encourages the use of SPF 15
or higher.

Cohen, Russell. "Tanning Trouble: Teens Are Using
Tanning Beds in Record Numbers." <u>Scholastic
Choices</u> 18 (2003): 23–28. Cohen warns that tanning
beds "can be just as dangerous as the sun's rays"
(23). The writer explains that tanning salons are not

Each entry gives full bibliographic information on the source—author, title, and publication data—as well as a brief description of the article or book.

Levenson 2

well regulated, so the amount of exposure can be really dangerous. The writer also explains how skin type affects tanning and the dangers of cancer.

Geller, Alan C., et al. "Use of Sunscreen, Sunburning Rates, and Tanning Bed Use among More Than 10,000 U.S. Children and Adolescents." <u>Pediatrics</u> 109 (2002): 1009–15. The objective of this study was to examine the psychosocial variables associated with teens seeking suntans. It collected data from questionnaires submitted by 10,079 boys and girls 12 to 18 years old. It concluded that many children are at risk for skin cancer because of failure to use sunscreen.

Segilia, Amanda. "Sunscreens, Suntans, and Sun Health." American Cancer Society. Interview. 13 June 2000. 4 June 2003 <http://www.intelihealth.com/ search>. This site features Harvard Medical School's Consumer Health Information. In this article, Amanda Segilia, a coordinator of Cancer Control Programs for the American Cancer Society, answers questions about tanning, including the use of sunscreen of SPF 15 or higher, use of suntan lotions, the effects of the sun, and the dangers of skin cancer.

"Skin Protection—My Teen Likes to Tan." St. Louis Children's Hospital. 2003. 3 June 2003 <http:// www.stlouischildrens.org/articles/ article_print.asp?ID=2670>. This site quotes Susan Mallory, the director of dermatology at St. Louis Children's Hospital, and registered nurse Ann Leonard, who both offer warnings against the use of tanning beds. Rather than damaging the skin with sun or tanning beds, the two experts suggest the use of tanning sprays or lotions.

Levenson 3

"Teens and the Sun." Health Watch. The U of Texas
    Southwestern Medical Center at Dallas. 29 July 2002.
    4 June 2003 <http://www3.utsouthwestern.edu/
    library/consumer/teen&sun02.htm>. This article
    warns teenagers against sun worship and skipping
    sunscreen. The experts suggest more public education
    and warnings. For example, teens should know that
    tanning damages the structure of the skin and
    promotes sagging skin and wrinkles in later life.
Zazinski, Janice. "A Legion of Ladies' Lesions." Research
    Briefs. Boston U. 11 Aug. 2000. 4 June 2003 <www.bu.edu/
    news/research/2000/8-11-suntans-chf.htm>. This
    article cites Dr. Marie-France Demierre, a professor
    of dermatology, who laments the use of tanning
    beds by young women. In truth, women are joining
    men in contracting and dying of melanoma, in great
    part because of tanning beds. Demierre and Zazinski
    warn youngsters against addiction to tanning beds
    and sun worship.

8g Using Your Notes to Write a Review of the Literature

The review of literature presents a set of summaries in essay form
for two purposes.

1. It helps you investigate the topic because it forces you to examine and then to record how each source addresses the problem.
2. It organizes and classifies the sources in some reasonable manner for the benefit of the reader.

Thus, you should relate each source to your central subject, and
you should group the sources according to their support of your thesis. For example, the brief review that follows explores the literature
on the subject of gender communication. It classifies the sources

under a progression of headings: the issues, the causes (both environmental and biological), the consequences for both men and women, and possible solutions.

You must also arrange the sources according to your selected categories or to fit your preliminary outline. Sometimes this task might be as simple as grouping those sources that favor a course or action and those that oppose it. In other cases—let's say it's a paper on Fitzgerald's *The Great Gatsby*—you may need to summarize sources by critics who examine Gatsby's character, others who study Daisy, and still others who write about Nick Carraway.

Like Kaci Holz, who wrote the paper below, you may wish to use side heads to identify your sections.

Holz 1

Kaci Holz

Dr. Bekus

April 23, 2003

English 1010

Gender Communication: A Review of the Literature

Several theories exist about different male and female communication styles. These ideas have been categorized below to establish the issues, shows causes for communication failures, the consequences for both men and women, and suggestions for possible solutions.

The Issues

Deborah Tannen, Ph.D., is a professor of sociolinguistics at Georgetown University. In her book <u>You Just Don't Understand: Men and Women in Conversation</u>, 1990, she claims there are basic gender patterns or stereotypes that can be found.

Tannen says that men participate in conversations to establish "a hierarchical social order," while women most often participate in conversations to establish "a network of connections" (Tannen, <u>Don't Understand</u> 24–25). She

The review of literature is an essay on the articles and books that address the writer's topic.

The writer uses the sources to establish the issues.

Holz 2

distinguishes between the way women use "rapport-talk" and the way men use "report-talk" (74).

In similar fashion, Susan Basow and Kimberly Rubenfeld, in "'Troubles Talk': Effects of Gender and Gender Typing," explore in detail the sex roles and how they determine and often control the speech of each gender. They notice that "women may engage in 'troubles talk' to enhance communication; men may avoid such talk to enhance autonomy and dominance" (186).

In addition, Phillip Yancey asserts that men and women "use conversation for quite different purposes" (71). He provides a 'no' answer to the question in his title, "Do Men and Women Speak the Same Language?" He claims that women converse to develop and maintain connections, while men converse to claim their position in the hierarchy they see around them. Yancey asserts that women are less likely to speak publicly than are men because women often perceive such speaking as putting oneself on display. A man, on the other hand, is usually comfortable with speaking publicly because that is how he establishes his status among others (Yancey 71).

Similarly, masculine people are "less likely than androgynous individuals to feel grateful for advice" (Basow and Rubenfeld 186). Julia T. Wood's book <u>Gendered Lives</u> claims that "male communication is characterized by assertion, independence, competitiveness, and confidence [while] female communication is characterized by deference, inclusivity, collaboration, and cooperation" (440). This list of differences describes why men and women have such opposing communication styles.

In another book, Tannen addresses the issue that boys, or men, "are more likely to take an oppositional stance toward other people and the world" and "are more likely to find opposition entertaining—to enjoy watching a good fight, or having one" (Tannen, <u>Argument</u> 166). Girls try to avoid fights.

Holz 3

Causes

Two different theories suggest causes for gender differences—the environment and biology.

<u>Environmental Causes</u>. Tammy James and Bethann Cinelli in 2003 mention, "The way men and women are raised contributes to differences in conversation and communication . . . " (41). Another author, Susan Witt, in "Parental Influence on Children's Socialization to Gender Roles," discusses the various findings that support the idea that parents have a great influence on their children during the development of their self-concept. She states, "Children learn at a very early age what it means to be a boy or a girl in our society" (253). She says that parents "[dress] infants in gender-specific colors, [give] gender-differentiated toys, and [expect] different behavior from boys and girls" (Witt 254).

Yancey notices a cultural gap, defining culture as "shared meaning" (68). He says, "Some problems come about because one spouse enters marriage with a different set of 'shared meanings' than the other" (69). The cultural gap affects the children. Yancey also talks about the "Battle of the Sexes" as seen in conflict between men and women. Reverting back to his 'childhood gender pattern' theory, Yancey claims, "Men, who grew up in a hierarchical environment, are accustomed to conflict. Women, concerned more with relationship and connection, prefer the role of peacemaker" (71).

Like Yancey, Deborah Tannen also addresses the fact that men and women often come from different worlds and different influences. She says, "Even if they grow up in the same neighborhood, on the same block, or in the same house, girls and boys grow up in different worlds of words" (Tannen, <u>Don't Understand</u> 43).

<u>Biological Causes</u>. Though Tannen often addresses the environmental issue in much of her research, she also looks at the biological issue in her book <u>The Argument</u>

The writer now uses the sources to explain the causes for communication failures.

Holz 4

Culture. Tannen states, "Surely a biological component plays a part in the greater use of antagonism among men, but cultural influence can override biological inheritance" (Tannen, Argument 205). She sums up the nature versus nurture issue by saying, "The patterns that typify women's and men's styles of opposition and conflict are the result of both biology and culture" (207).

Lillian Glass, another linguistics researcher, has a 1992 book called He Says, She Says: Closing the Communication Gap between the Sexes. Glass addresses the issue that different hormones found in men and women's bodies make them act differently and therefore communicate differently. She also discusses how brain development has been found to relate to sex differences.

Judy Mann says, "Most experts now believe that what happens to boys and girls is a complex interaction between slight biological differences and tremendously powerful social forces that begin to manifest themselves the minute the parents find out whether they are going to have a boy or a girl" (qtd. in McCluskey 6).

Consequences of Gender Differences

The writer now uses the sources to explain the consequence of communication failures on both men and women.

Now that we have looked at different styles of gender communication and possible causes of gender communication, let us look at the possible results. Michelle Weiner-Davis is a marriage and family therapist who wrote the best seller Divorce Busting. She says to the point, "Ignorance about the differences in gender communication has been a major contributor to divorce" (qtd. in Warren 106).

Through various studies, Tannen has concluded that men and women have different purposes for engaging in communication. In the open forum that Deborah Tannen and Robert Bly gave in New York in 1993, Tannen (on videotape) explains the different ways men and women handle communication throughout the day. She explains

Holz 5

that a man constantly talks during his workday in order to impress those around him and to establish his status in the office. At home he wants peace and quiet. On the other hand, a woman is constantly cautious and guarded about what she says during her workday. Women try hard to avoid confrontation and avoid offending anyone with their language. So when a woman comes home from work she expects to be able to talk freely without having to guard her words. The consequence? The woman expects conversation, but the man is tired of talking.

Solutions

Answers for better gender communication seem elusive. What can be done about this apparent gap in communication between genders? In his article published in <u>Leadership</u>, Jeffrey Arthurs offers the obvious suggestion that women should make an attempt to understand the male model of communication and that men should make an attempt to understand the female model of communication.

The writer now depends on the sources to provide possible solutions.

However, in his article "Speaking across the Gender Gap," David Cohen mentions that experts didn't think it would be helpful to teach men to communicate more like women and women to communicate more like men. This attempt would prove unproductive because it would go against what men and women have been taught since birth. Rather than change the genders to be more like one another, we could simply try to "understand" each other better.

In addition, Richard Weaver makes this observation: "The idea that women should translate their experiences into the male code in order to express themselves effectively . . . is an outmoded, inconsistent, subservient notion that should no longer be given credibility in modern society" (439). He suggests three things we can change: 1.) Change

Holz 6

the norm by which leadership success is judged, 2.)
Redefine what we mean by power, and 3.) Become more
sensitive to the places and times when inequity and
inequality occur (Weaver 439). Similarly, Yancey offers
advice to help combat "cross-cultural" fights. He suggests:
1.) Identify your fighting style, 2.) Agree on rules of
engagement, and 3.) Identify the real issue behind the
conflict (Yancey 71).

McCluskey claims men and women need honest
communication that shows respect, and they must "manage
conflict in a way that maintains the relationship and gets
the job done" (5). She says, "To improve relationships and
interactions between men and women, we must
acknowledge the differences that do exist, understand how
they develop, and discard dogma about what are the 'right'
roles of women and men" (5).

Obviously, differences exist in the way men and women
communicate, whether caused by biological and/or
environmental factors. We can consider the possible causes,
the consequences, and possible solutions. Using this
knowledge, we should be able to more accurately interpret
communication between the genders.

Holz 7

Works Cited

Arthurs, Jeffrey. "He Said, She Heard: Any Time You
    Speak to Both Men and Women, You're Facing
    Cross-Cultural Communication." <u>Leadership</u> 23.1
    (2002): 49. Expanded Academic Index. Austin Peay
    State U., Woodward Lib. 22 Sept 2003
    <http://www.galegroup.com/search>.

Basow, Susan A., and Kimberly Rubenfeld. "'Troubles
    Talk': Effects of Gender and Gender Typing." <u>Sex
    Roles: A Journal of Research</u> (2003): 183– .
    Expanded Academic Index. Austin Peay State U.,
    Woodward Lib. 24 Apr. 2003 <http://
    web5.infotrac.galegroup.com/search>.

Cohen, David. "Speaking across the Gender Gap." <u>New
    Scientist</u> 131.1783 (1991): 36. Expanded Academic
    Index. Austin Peay State U, Woodward Lib. 28 Sept
    2003.

<u>Deborah Tannen & Robert Bly: Men & Women Talking
    Together</u>. New York Open Center. Videocassette.
    Mystic Fire Video, 1993.

Glass, Lillian. <u>He Says, She Says: Closing the
    Communication Gap between the Sexes</u>. New York:
    G.P. Putnam's Sons, 1992.

James, Tammy, and Bethann Cinelli. "Exploring Gender-
    Based Communication Styles." <u>Journal of School
    Health</u> 73 (2003): 41–42.

McCluskey, Karen Curnow. "Gender at Work." <u>Public
    Management</u> 79.5 (1997): 5–10.

Tannen, Deborah. <u>The Argument Culture: Moving from
    Debate to Dialogue</u>. New York: Random House,
    1998.

– – –. <u>You Just Don't Understand: Women and Men in
    Conversation</u>. New York: Ballantine, 1990.

Warren, Andrea. "How to Get Him to Listen." <u>Ladies'
    Home Journal</u> 113 (Mar. 1996): 106.

The separate Works Cited page gives full information on each source cited in the paper.

Holz 8

Weaver, Richard L. "Leadership for the Future: A New
Set of Priorities." <u>Vital Speeches of the Day</u> 61
(1995): 438–41.

Witt, Susan D. "Parental Influence on Children's
Socialization to Gender Roles." <u>Adolescence</u> 32
(1997): 253.

Woods, Julia T. <u>Gendered Lives</u>. San Francisco:
Wadsworth, 2002.

Yancey, Phillip. "Do Men and Women Speak the Same
Language?" <u>Marriage Partnership</u> 10 (1993): 68–73.

9

Drafting the Paper in an Academic Style

As you draft your paper, you should adopt an academic style that reflects your discipline, as discussed next in section 9a. Present a fair, balanced treatment of the subject. Mentioning opposing viewpoints early in a report gives you something to work against and may strengthen your conclusion. Keep in mind that negative findings have value and should be reported even if they contradict your original hypothesis (see page 107 for more on the logic and ethics of a presentation).

Three principles for drafting may serve your needs:

- *Be practical.* Write portions of the paper when you are ready, skipping over sections of your outline. Leave plenty of space for notes and corrections.
- *Be uninhibited.* Write without fear or delay because initial drafts are attempts to get words on the page rather than to create a polished document.
- *Be conscientious about citations.* Cite the names of the sources in your notes and text, enclose quotations, and preserve page numbers to the sources.

This chapter will help you find the style necessary for your field of study, focus your argument, and build the introduction, body, and conclusion.

9a Writing for Your Field of Study

Each discipline has its own special language, style of expression, and manuscript format. You will, in time, learn fully the style for your college major. Meanwhile, we can identify a few characteristics to guide your writing styles for papers in the humanities, the social sciences, and the physical sciences.

Academic Style in the Humanities

Writing in one of the humanities requires you to adopt a certain style, as shown in the following example, which is written in the CMS footnote style.

> Organ and tissue donation is the gift of life. Each year many people confront health problems due to diseases or congenital birth defects. Tom Taddonia explains that tissues such as skin, veins, and valves can be used to correct congenital defects, blindness, visual impairment, trauma, burns, dental defects, arthritis, cancer, vascular and heart disease.[8] Steve Barnill says, "More than 400 people each month receive the gift of sight through yet another type of tissue donation—corneal transplants. In many cases, donors unsuitable for organ donation are eligible for tissue donation."[9] Barnill notes that tissues are now used in orthopedic surgery, cardiovascular surgery, plastic surgery, dentistry, and podiatry.[10] Even so, not enough people are willing to donate organs and tissues.

Writing in the humanities often displays these characteristics:

- Preoccupation with the quality of life, of art, of ideas (as shown in the first sentence and as echoed in the final sentence)
- Personal involvement on ethical standards
- Use of the present tense to indicate that this problem is an enduring one for humans of past ages as well as the present and the future
- Use of the CMS footnote style or the MLA style
- Discussion of theory as supported by the literature

Academic Style in the Social Sciences

Let us look at how a social science student might write the same passage in APA style.

> Organ and tissue donation has been identified as a social as well as medical problem in the United States. On one side, people have confronted serious problems in securing organs and tissue to correct health problems; on the other, people have demonstrated a reluctance to donate their organs. This need has been identified by Taddonia (2001), Barnill (1999), Ruskin (2000), and others. This hypothesis remains: People

are reluctant to sign the donor cards. Consequently, this study will survey a random set of 1,000 persons who have drivers' licenses. The tabulations will indicate reasons for signing or not signing for donation. Further investigation can then be conducted to determine ways of increasing participation by potential donors.

As shown, writing in the social sciences typically displays these characteristics:

- An objective approach to the topic without signs of personal commitment
- A scientific plan for examining a hypothesis
- Preference for the passive voice
- Minimal quotations from the sources, anticipating that readers will examine the literature for themselves
- An indication of the study's purpose and/or a general plan for empirical research
- Use of APA style for documenting the sources
- Use of past tense or the present perfect tense in references to the source material
- Awareness that this research will prompt further study

Academic Style in the Physical and Medical Sciences

Now let us look at how a medical student might write on this same topic in CSE number style:

Taddonia (1) has shown that human tissue can be used to correct many defects. Barnill (2) showed that more than 400 people receive corneal transplants each month. Yet the health profession needs more donors. It has been shown (3–6) that advanced care directives by patients with terminal illnesses would improve the donation of organs and tissue and relieve relatives of making any decision. Patients have been encouraged to complete organ donation cards (7) as well as to sign living wills (5, 8), special powers of attorney (5), and DNR (Do Not Resuscitate) Orders (5, 8). It is encouraged that advanced care directives become standard for the terminally ill.

Scientific or medical writing, like the passage above, typically displays some of these characteristics.

- An objective approach to the topic without signs of personal commitment

- A search for a professional position (i.e., on organ donation)
- A preference for the passive voice and for past tense verbs
- A preference for the CSE number system or, in some cases, the name-year system (see the samples above)
- A reluctance to quote from the sources
- A willingness to let a number represent the literature that will be cited with full documentation on the page of references

9b Focusing Your Argument

Your writing style in the research paper must be factual, but it should also reflect your thinking on the topic. You will be able to draft your paper more quickly if you focus on the central issue(s). Each paragraph should build on and amplify your primary claim.

Persuading, Inquiring, and Negotiating

Establishing a purpose for writing is one way to focus your argument. Do you wish to persuade, inquire, negotiate? Most research papers make an inquiry.

Persuasion means that you wish to convince the reader that your position is valid and, perhaps, to take action. For example:

> Research has shown that homeowners and wild animals cannot live together in harmony. Thus, we need to establish green zones in every city of this country to control the sprawl in urban areas and to protect a segment of the natural habitat for the animals.

Inquiry is an exploratory approach to a problem in which you examine the issues without the insistence of persuasion. It is a truth-seeking adventure. You often must examine, test, or observe in order to discuss the implications of the research. For example:

> Many suburban home dwellers complain that deer, raccoons, and other wild animals ravage their gardens, flowerbeds, and garbage cans; however, the animals were there first. This study will examine the problem in one subdivision of 142 homes. How have animals been affected by the intrusion of human beings? How have homeowners been harassed by the animals? The research will examine each side of the conflict by interviews will homeowners and observation of the animals.

Negotiation is a search for a solution. It means that you attempt to resolve a conflict by inventing options or a mediated solution. For example:

> Suburban neighbors need to find ways to embrace the wild animals that have been displaced rather than voice anger at the animals or the county government. Research has shown that green zones and wilderness trails would solve some of the problems; however, such a solution would require serious negotiations with real estate developers, who want to use every square foot of every development.

Maintaining a Focus with Ethical and Logical Appeals

As an objective writer, you must examine the problem, make your claim, and provide supporting evidence. Moderation of your voice, even during argument, suggests control of the situation, both emotionally and intellectually. Your voice alerts the audience to your point of view in two ways:

Ethical appeal. If you project the image of one who knows and cares about the topic, the reader will recognize and respect your deep interest in the subject and the way you have carefully crafted your argument. The reader will also appreciate your attention to research conventions.

Logical appeal. For readers to believe in your position, you must provide sufficient evidence in the form of statistical data, paraphrases, and direct quotations from authorities on the subject.

The issue of organ donation, for example, elicits different reactions. Some people argue from the logical position that organs are available and should be used to help people in need. Others argue from the ethical position that organs might be harvested prematurely or that organ donation violates religious principles. As a writer, you must balance your ethical and logical appeals to your readers.

Focusing the Final Thesis Sentence or Hypothesis

Refining your thesis may keep your paper on track. A thesis statement expresses the theory you hope to support with evidence and arguments. A hypothesis is a theory you hope to prove by investigating, testing, or observing. Both the thesis and the hypothesis are propositions you want to maintain, analyze, and prove. A final thesis statement or hypothesis performs three tasks:

1. Establishes a claim to control and focus the entire paper.
2. Provides unity and a sense of direction.
3. Specifies to the reader the point of the research.

For example, one student started with the topic *exorbitant tuition,* narrowed it to the phrase "tuition fees put parents in debt," and ultimately crafted this thesis:

> The exorbitant tuition at America's colleges is forcing out the poor and promoting an elitist class.

This statement focuses the argument on the effects of high fees on enrollment. The student must prove the assertion by gathering and tabulating statistics.

Questions focus the thesis. If you have trouble finding a claim or argument, ask yourself a few questions. One of the answers might serve as the thesis or the hypothesis.

- What is the point of my research?

  HYPOTHESIS: A delicate balance of medicine, diet, and exercise can control diabetes mellitus.

- Can I tell the reader anything new or different?

  HYPOTHESIS: Most well water in Rutherford county is unsafe for drinking.

- Do I have a solution to the problem?

  THESIS: Public support for "safe" houses will provide a haven for children who are abused by their parents.

- Do I have a new slant and new approach to the issue?

  HYPOTHESIS: Poverty, not greed, forces many youngsters into a life of crime.

- Should I take the minority view of this matter?

  THESIS: Give credit where it is due: Custer may have lost the battle at Little Bighorn, but Crazy Horse and his men, with inspiration from Sitting Bull, <u>won</u> the battle.

- Will an enthymeme serve my purpose by making a claim in a *because* clause?

  ENTHYMEME: Sufficient organ and tissue donation, enough to satisfy the demand, remains almost impossible because negative myths and religious concerns dominate the minds of many people.

C H E C K L I S T

Writing the Final Thesis or Hypothesis

You should be able to answer *yes* to each question below:

- Does the thesis or hypothesis express your position in a full, declarative statement that is not a question, not a statement of purpose, and not merely a topic?
- Does it limit the subject to a narrow focus that grows out of research?
- Does it establish an investigation, interpretation, or theoretical presentation?
- Does it point forward to your findings and a discussion of the implications in your conclusion?

Key words focus the thesis or the hypothesis. Use the important words from your notes and rough outline to refine your thesis sentence. For example, during your reading of several novels or short stories by Flannery O'Connor, you might have jotted down certain repetitions of image, theme, or character. The key words might be *death, ironic moments of humor, hysteria and passion, human shortcomings,* or other issues that O'Connor repeatedly explored. These concrete ideas might point you toward a general thesis:

> The tragic endings of Flannery O'Connor's stories depict desperate people coming face to face with their own shortcomings.

Change your thesis but not your hypothesis. Be willing to abandon your preliminary thesis if research leads you to new and different issues. However, a hypothesis *cannot* be adjusted or changed. It will be proved true, partially true, or untrue. Your negative findings have value, for you will have disproved the hypothesis so others need not duplicate your research. For example, the hypothesis might assert: "Industrial pollution is seeping into water tables and traveling many miles into neighboring well water of Thompson county." Your report may prove the truth of the hypothesis, but it may not. It may only establish a probability and the need for additional research.

9c Designing an Academic Title

A clearly expressed title, like a good thesis sentence, focuses your writing and keeps you on course. Although writing a final title may not be feasible until the paper is written, a preliminary title can provide specific words of identification to help you stay focused. For example, one writer began with this title: "Diabetes." Then, to be more specific, the writer added another word: "Diabetes Management." As research developed and she recognized the role of medicine, diet, and exercise for victims, she refined the title even more: "Diabetes Management: A Delicate Balance of Medicine, Diet, and Exercise." Thereby, she and her readers had a clear idea that the paper was about three methods of managing the disease.

Long titles are standard in scholarly writing. Consider the following examples:

1. Subject, colon, and focusing phrase:

Organ and Tissue Donation and Transplantation: Myths, Ethical Issues, and Lives Saved

2. Subject, focusing prepositional phrase:

Prayer at School-Related Activities

3. Subject, colon, type of study:

Black Dialect in Maya Angelou's Poetry: A Language Study

4. Subject, colon, focusing question:

AIDS: Where Did It Come From?

5. Subject, comparative study:

Religious Imagery in N. Scott Momaday's <u>The Names</u> and Heronimous Storm's <u>Seven Arrows</u>

For placement of the title, see one of these examples: MLA, pages 95 and 141; APA, page 158; CMS, page 175; CSE, page 184.

9d Drafting the Paper

As you begin drafting your research report, work systematically through a preliminary plan or outline to keep order as your notes expand your research (see pages 73–79 for models of organization). Use your notes, photocopies, downloaded material, and research journal to transfer materials directly into the text, remembering always to provide citations to borrowed information. Do not quote an entire paragraph unless it is crucial to your discussion and cannot be easily reduced to a summary. In addition, be conscious of basic writing conventions, as described next.

Writing with Unity and Coherence

Unity refers to exploring one topic in depth to give your writing a single vision. With unity, each paragraph carefully expands on a single aspect of the narrowed subject. *Coherence* connects the parts logically by:

- repetition of key words and sentence structures
- the judicious use of pronouns and synonyms
- the effective placement of transitional words and phrases (e.g., *also, furthermore, therefore, in addition,* and *thus*)

Writing in the Proper Tense

Verb tense often distinguishes a paper in the humanities from one in the natural and social sciences. Use the past tense in the social sciences and the physical sciences (see the examples on pages 104–06). Use the present tense in the humanities. Both the MLA style and the CMS footnote style require the present tense to cite an author's work (e.g., "Patel *explains*" or "the work of Scogin and Roberts *shows*"). The ideas and the words of the writers remain in print and continue to be true in the universal present. Therefore, when writing a paper in the humanities, use the historical present tense, as shown here:

> "It was the best of times, it was the worst of times," writes Charles Dickens about the eighteenth century.

> Johnson argues that sociologist Norman Wayman has a "narrow-minded view of clerics and their role in the community" (64).

Using the Language of the Discipline

Every discipline and every topic has its own vocabulary. Therefore, while reading and taking notes, jot down words and phrases relevant to your research study. Get comfortable with them so you can use them effectively. For example, a child abuse topic requires the language of sociology and psychology, thereby demanding an acquaintance with the following terms:

social worker	maltreatment	aggressive behavior
poverty levels	behavioral patterns	incestuous relations
stress	hostility	battered child
formative years	recurrence	guardians

Many writers create a terminology list to strengthen their command of appropriate nouns and verbs for the subject in question.

Using Source Material to Enhance Your Writing

Readers want to see your thoughts and ideas on a subject. For this reason, a paragraph should seldom contain source material only; it must contain a topic sentence to establish a point for the research evidence. Every paragraph should explain, analyze, and support a thesis, not merely string together a set of quotations. The following passage effectively cites two sources.

> Two factors that have played a part in farm land becoming drought prone are "light, sandy soil and soils with high alkalinity" (Boughman 234). In response, Bjornson says that drought resistant plants exist along parts of the Mediterranean Sea. Thus, hybrids of these plants may serve Texas farmers (34).

The short passage weaves the sources effectively into a whole, uses the sources as a natural extension of the discussion, and cites each source separately and appropriately.

Writing in the Third Person

Write your paper with third-person narration that avoids "I believe" or "It is my opinion." Rather than saying, "I think television violence affects children," drop the opening two words and say, "Television violence affects children." Readers will understand that the statement is your thought and one that you will defend with evidence.

Writing with the Passive Voice in an Appropriate Manner

The passive voice is often less forceful than an active verb. However, research writers sometimes need to use the passive voice verb, as shown here:

> Forty-three students of a third-grade class at Barksdale School were observed for two weeks.

This usage of the passive voice is fairly standard in the social sciences and the natural or applied sciences. The passive voice is preferred because it keeps the focus on the subject of the research, not the writer (you would not want to say, "I observed the students").

Placing Graphics Effectively in a Research Essay

Use graphics to support your text. Most computers allow you to create tables, line graphs, and pie charts as well as diagrams, maps, and original designs. You may also import tables and illustrations from your sources. Place these graphics as close as possible to the parts of the text to which they relate. It is acceptable to use full-color art if your printer prints in color; however, use black for the captions and date. Place a full-page graphic on a separate sheet after making a textual reference to it (e.g., "see Table 7"). Place graphics in an appendix when you have several complex items that might distract the reader from your textual message.

See pages 190–195 for help with designing and documenting illustrations.

Avoiding Sexist and Biased Language

The best writers exercise caution against words that may stereotype any person, regardless of gender, race, nationality, creed, age, or disability. The following are guidelines to help you avoid discriminatory language:

Age. Review the accuracy of your statement. It is appropriate to use *boy* and *girl* for children of high school age and under. *Young man* and *young woman* or *male adolescent* and *female adolescent* can be appropriate, but *teenager* carries a certain bias. Avoid *elderly* as a noun; use *older persons.*

Gender. Gender is a term used culturally to identify men and women within their social groups. *Sex* tends to refer to a biological factor (see below for a discussion of sexual orientation).

- Use plural subjects so that nonspecific, plural pronouns are grammatically correct. For example, you may specify that Judy Jones maintains *her* lab equipment in sterile condition or indicate that technicians, in general, maintain *their* own equipment.
- Reword the sentence so a pronoun is unnecessary, as in *The doctor prepared the necessary surgical equipment without interference.*
- Use pronouns that denote gender only when necessary when gender has been previously established, as in *Mary, as a new laboratory technician, must learn to maintain her equipment in sterile condition.*
- The use of *woman* and *female* as adjectives varies. Use *woman* or *women* in most instances (e.g., *a woman's intuition*) and use *female* for species and statistics, (e.g., *four female subjects*). Avoid the use of *lady,* as in *lady pilot.*
- The first mention of a person requires the full name (e.g., Ernest Hemingway, Joan Didion) and thereafter requires

the use of the surname only (e.g., Hemingway, Didion). In general, avoid formal titles (e.g., Dr., Gen., Mrs., Ms., Lt., Prof.). Avoid their equivalents in other languages (e.g., Mme, Dame, Monsieur).

- Avoid *man and wife* or *7 men and 16 females*. Keep terms parallel by matching *husband and wife* or *man and woman* and *7 male rats and 16 female rats*.

Sexual Orientation. The term *sexual orientation* is preferred to the term *sexual preference*. It is preferable to use *lesbians* and *gay men* rather than *homosexuals*. The terms *heterosexual, homosexual,* and *bisexual* can be used to describe both the identity and the behavior of subjects—that is, as adjectives.

Ethnic and Racial Identity. Some persons prefer the term *Black*, others prefer *African American,* and still others prefer *a person of color.* The terms *Negro* and *Afro-American* are now dated and not appropriate. Use *Black* and *White*, not the lowercase *black* and *white*. In like manner, some individuals may prefer *Hispanic* or *Latino*. Use the term *Asian* or *Asian American* rather than *Oriental*. *Native American* is a broad term that includes *Samoans, Hawaiians,* and *American Indians*. A good rule of thumb is to use a person's nationality when it is known (*Mexican, Canadian, Comanche,* or *Nigerian*).

Disability. In general, place people first, not their disability. Rather than *disabled person* or *retarded child* say *person who has scoliosis* or *a child with Down syndrome*. Avoid saying *a challenged person* or *a special child* in favor of *a person with* or *a child with*. Remember that a *disability* is a physical quality while a *handicap* is a limitation that might be imposed by external factors, such as stairs or poverty or social attitudes.

 ## Creating an Introduction, Body, and Conclusion

Writing the Introduction

Use the first few paragraphs of your paper to establish the nature of your study.

SUBJECT: Does your introduction identify your specific topic, and then define, limit, and narrow it to one issue?

BACKGROUND: Does your introduction provide relevant historical data or discuss a few key sources that touch on your specific issue?

PROBLEM: Does your introduction identify a problem and explain the complications your research paper will explore or resolve?

THESIS: Does your introduction use your thesis sentence or hypothesis within the first few paragraphs to establish the direction of the study and to point your readers toward your eventual conclusions?

How you work these essential elements into the beginning of your paper depends on your style of writing. They need not appear in this order, nor should you cram all these items into a short, opening paragraph. Feel free to write a long introduction by using more than one of these techniques:

Open with your thesis statement or hypothesis.
Open with a quotation.
Relate your topic to the well known.
Provide background information.
Review the literature.
Provide a brief summary.
Define key terms.
Supply data, statistics, and special evidence.
Take exception to critical views.
Use an anecdote as a hook to draw your reader into the essay.

The following sample of an introduction gives background information, establishes a persuasive position, reviews key literature, takes exception, gives key terms, and offers a thesis.

John Berendt's popular and successful novel <u>Midnight in the Garden of Good and Evil</u> skillfully presents the unpredictable twists and turns of a landmark murder case set under the moss-hung live oaks of Savannah, Georgia. While it is written as a novel, the nonfiction account of this tragic murder case reveals the intriguing and sometimes deranged relationships that thrive in a town where everyone knows everyone else. However, the mystique of the novel does not lie with the murder case but with the collection of unusual and often complex characters, including a voodoo priestess, a young southern gigolo, and a black drag queen (e.g., Bilkin, Miller, and especially Carson, who describes the people of Savannah as "a type of Greek chorus" [14]). Berendt's success lies in his carefully crafted characterization.

Writing the Body of the Research Paper

When writing the body, you should keep in mind three elements:

ANALYSIS:	Classify the major issues of the study and provide a careful analysis of each in defense of your thesis.
PRESENTATION:	Provide well-reasoned statements at the beginning of your paragraphs and supply evidence of support with proper documentation.
PARAGRAPHS:	Offer a variety of paragraphs to compare, show process, narrate the history of the subject, and show causes.

Use these techniques to build substantive paragraphs for your paper:

Relate a time sequence.
Compare or contrast issues, the views of experts, and nature of literary characters.
Develop cause and effect.
Issue a call to action.
Define key terminology.
Show a process.
Ask questions and provide answers.
Cite evidence from source materials.
Explain the methods used and the design of the study.
Present the results of the investigation with data, statistics, and graphics.

The following paragraph in MLA style demonstrates the use of several techniques—an overview of the problem, citing a source, comparing issues, cause and effect, key terms, and process.

To burn or not to burn the natural forests in the national parks is the question. The pyrophobic public voices its protests while environmentalists praise the rejuvenating effects of a good forest fire. It is difficult to convince people that not all fire is bad. The public has visions of Smokey the Bear campaigns and mental images of Bambi and Thumper fleeing the roaring flames. Chris Bolgiano explains that federal policy evolved slowly "from the basic impulse to douse all fires immediately to a sophisticated decision matrix based on the functions of any given unit of land" (23). Bolgiano declares that "timber production, grazing, recreation, and wilderness preservation elicit different fire-management approaches" (23).

Writing the Conclusion of the Paper

The conclusion is not a summary; it is a discussion of beliefs and findings based on your reasoning and on the evidence and results you presented. Select appropriate items from this list.

THESIS: Reaffirm the thesis sentence, the hypothesis, or the central mission of your study. If appropriate, give a statement in support or nonsupport of an original enthymeme or hypothesis.

JUDGMENT: Discuss and interpret the findings. Give answers. Now is the time to draw inferences, emphasize a theory, and find relevance in the results.

DIRECTIVES: Based on the theoretical implications of the study, offer suggestions for action and for new research.

DISCUSSION: Discuss the implications of your findings from testing or observation.

Use these techniques to write the conclusion:

Restate the thesis and reach beyond it.
Close with an effective quotation.
Return the focus of a literary study to the author.
Compare the past to the present.
Offer a directive or a solution.
Give a call to action.
Discuss the implications of your findings.

This next example in CSE style (see Chapter 13) discusses test results of one student's empirical study.

The results of this experiment were similar to expectations, but perhaps the statistical significance, because of the small subject size, was biased toward the delayed conditions of the curve. Barker (14) and Peay (3) have addressed this point. The subjects were not truly representative of the total population because of their prior exposure to test procedures (e.g., see 2, 3, and 7). Another factor that may have affected the curves was the presentation of the data. The images on the screen were available for five seconds, and that amount of time may have enabled the subjects to store each image effectively. If the time period for each image were reduced to one or two seconds, there could be lower recall scores, thereby reducing the differences between the control group and the experimental group.

9f Revising the Rough Draft

Once you have the complete paper in a rough draft, the serious business of editing begins. First, you should revise your paper on a global scale, moving blocks of material around to the best advantage and into the proper format. Second, edit the draft with a line-by-line examination of wording and technical excellence. Third, proofread the final version to assure that your words are spelled correctly and the text is grammatically sound.

Revision can turn a passable paper into an excellent one. Revise the manuscript on a global scale by looking at its overall design. Do the introduction, body, and conclusion have substance? Do the paragraphs maintain the flow of your central proposition? Does the paper fulfill the requirements of the academic model?

Editing before Printing the Final Manuscript

Global revision is complemented by careful editing of paragraphs, sentences, and individual words. Travel through the paper to study your citation of the sources. Confirm that you have properly quoted or paraphrased each cited source. Check spelling with both the computer and your own visual examination. Here are eight additional tasks:

1. Cut phrases and sentences that do not advance your main ideas or that merely repeat what your sources have already stated.
2. Determine that coordinated, balanced ideas are appropriately expressed and that minor ideas are properly subordinated.
3. Change most of your *to be* verbs (is, are, was) to stronger active verbs.
4. Maintain the present tense in most verbs unless you writing in APA or CSE styles.
5. Convert passive structures to active unless you want to emphasize the subject, not the actor (see page 112).
6. Confirm that you have introduced paraphrases and quotations so they flow smoothly into your text.
7. Use formal, academic style, and be on guard against clusters of little monosyllabic words that fail to advance ideas.

   Good: Findings by Marshall (2003) and Fields (2004) confirm class size as one indicator of student success.

Wordy: In the writings of two authorities, Marshall (2003) and Fields (2004), the number of students in a classroom determines the success of the academic performance.

Examine your wording for its effectiveness in the context of your subject (see page 111).

8. Examine your paragraphs for transitions that move the reader effectively from one paragraph to the next.

Using the Computer to Edit Your Text

Some software programs examine your grammar and mechanics, look for parentheses that you opened but never closed, find unpaired quotation marks, flag passive verbs, question your spelling, and mark other items for your correction. Pay attention to the caution flags raised by this type of program. After a software program examines the style of your manuscript, you should revise and edit the text to improve stylistic weaknesses. Remember, it is your paper, not the computer's.

Participating in Peer Review

Peer review has two sides. First, it means handing your paper to a friend or classmate, asking for opinions and suggestions. Second, it means reviewing a classmate's research paper. You can learn by reviewing as well as by writing. Your instructor may supply a peer review sheet, or you can use the accompanying checklist. Criticize the paper constructively on each point.

C H E C K L I S T

Peer Review

1. Are the subject and the accompanying issues introduced early?

2. Is the writer's critical approach to the problem stated clearly in a thesis sentence? Is it placed effectively in the introduction?

3. Do the paragraphs of the body have individual unity—that is, does each paragraph develop an important idea and only one idea? Does each paragraph relate to the thesis?

4. Are sources introduced, usually with the name of the expert, and then cited by a page number in parentheses? Keep in mind that Internet sources rarely have page numbers.

5. Is it clear where a paraphrase begins and where it ends?

6. Are the sources relevant to the argument?

7. Does the writer weave quotations into the text effectively while avoiding long quotations that look more like filler than substance?

8. Does the conclusion arrive at a resolution about the central issue?

9. Does the title describe clearly what the writer put in the body of the research paper?

Proofreading

Print a hard copy of your manuscript. Proofread this final version with great care.

CHECKLIST

Proofreading

1. Check for errors in sentence structure, spelling, and punctuation.

2. Check for hyphenation and word division. Remember that no words should be hyphenated at the ends of lines.

3. Recheck the accuracy of all direct quotations. Check for opening and closing quotation marks.

4. Double-check in-text citations to be certain each is correct and that each source is listed on your Works Cited page.

5. Double-check the format—the title page, margins, spacing, content notes, and many other elements. These stipulations are explained in the chapters on using MLA, CMS, APA, and CSE styles and in the glossary on page 196.

10

Using MLA Style

This chapter is devoted to the style set by the Modern Language Association (MLA), a group of professional scholars who set the standards for research writing in literature, English usage, and the foreign languages.

10a Blending Sources into Your Writing

The MLA style requires the full name of a source on first mention and the last name thereafter.

> Ralph Templeton examines in depth the animal imagery in Thomas Hardy's novels (53–124).

However, mention the last name only in parenthetical citations, even the first.

> One source has examined in depth the animal imagery in Thomas Hardy's novels (Templeton 53–124).

Quotations, paraphrases, and summaries should support your topic sentences, and they contribute coherence if they extend a paragraph's argument. A collection of random quotations is unacceptable. Notice how the following example introduces the idea of executive power and develops it with citations.

> The power of the executive mansion began in November 1801 when John Adams, accompanied by a single secretary and servant, entered "the unfinished White House that smelled of plaster and paint" (Olson 23). One of his first tasks was to write a letter to his wife, Abigail. According to Richard Striker, voters must always consider the words that Adams

used on that first day in the White House: "May none but
honest and wise men ever rule under this roof" (qtd. in
Striker 78). At no other time are these simple words more
compelling than when the nation considers candidates for
the highest office during an election.

Identifying the Author and a Page Number

Sometimes you need no parenthetical citation.

The women of Thomas Hardy's novels are the special focus
of three essays by Nancy Norris, Judith Mitchell, and
James Scott.

Usually, you should introduce a quotation or a paraphrase with
the author's name and close it with a page number, placed in parentheses.

Herbert Norfleet states that the use of video games by
children improves their hand and eye coordination (45).

Sometimes, notes at the end of a quotation make it expeditious
to place the page number immediately after the name.

Rizarrio (34) urges businesses to "stop the ridiculous practice
of <u>overlighting</u> with brighter signs and entrance lights"
(emphasis added).

When no author is shown on a title page, cite the title of an article, the name of the magazine, the name of the bulletin or book, or
the name of the publishing organization.

The mutual fund market has shown a significant increase in
activity during the past ten years and has yet to reach its
peak (Annual Report 12).

Identifying Nonprint Sources That Have No Page Number

Mention the type of source so readers will not expect a page
number.

Fuller's lecture emphasized that too many individuals
"consider themselves invulnerable and much too crafty to be
caught shoplifting—until they are actually caught."

Identifying Internet Sources

Include a paragraph number or a page number *only* if the author of the Internet article provided it.

> Hershel Winthop interprets Hawthorne's stories as the search for holiness in a corrupt Puritan society (par. 16).

Citing Indirect Sources

Sometimes the writer of a book or article quotes another person from an interview or personal correspondence. If you want to use such a quotation, conform to this next example, which cites the person making the statement (Greenburg) and then cites the source where the material was found (Peterson).

> After students get beyond middle school, they begin to resent interference by their parents, especially in school activities. They need some space from Mom and Dad. Martin Greenburg says, "The interventions can be construed by the adolescent as negative, overburdening and interfering with the child's ability to care for himself" (qtd. in Peterson 9A).

Without the reference to Peterson, it would be difficult to find the article in the Works Cited list; without the reference to Greenburg, readers would assume that Peterson had spoken the words.

Citing Material from Textbooks and Large Anthologies

If you quote from a textbook anthology, cite only the author and the page of the text. The Works Cited entry will identify the anthology.

> In "How to Tell a True War Story," Tim O'Brien reminds readers that "war is hell, but that's not the half of it, because war is also mystery and terror and adventure and courage and discovery and holiness and pity and despair and longing and love" (465).

Adding Extra Information to In-text Citations

A detailed citation, such as "(Great Expectations 681; chap. 4)" helps the reader locate the passage. The next citation shows several authors listed in one citation:

> Several sources have suggested that Nashville, Tennessee, the Music City, borders between reality and fantasy as the

last place where the American dream of country singers can become reality (Bales 98–99; Riggins 55; Earley 261–63).

10b Punctuating Citations Properly and Consistently

Keep parenthetical citations outside quotation marks but inside the final period, as shown here:

> Yaffe says what we talk about when we talk about jazz is "the provenance of metaphor: Ellison's Invisible Man looking toward Louis Armstrong as his muse" (123).

HINT: Do not use *p.* or *pp.* with the page number(s) when using the MLA style.

The example below shows how to place commas and quotation marks.

> "Modern advertising," says Rachel Murphy, "not only creates a marketplace, it determines values." She adds, "I resist the advertiser's argument that they 'awaken, not create desires'" (192).

Both semicolons and colons go outside quotation marks.

> Brian Sutton-Smith says, "Adults don't worry whether their toys are educational" (64); nevertheless, parents want to keep their children in a learning mode.

When a question mark or an exclamation point is a part of the quotation, keep it inside the closing quotation mark.

> Thompson (16) passionately shouted to union members, "We can bring order into our lives even though we face hostility from every quarter!"

Retain question marks and exclamation points when the quotation begins a sentence.

> "We face hostility from every quarter!" declared the union leader.

Place question marks inside the closing quotation mark when they are part of the original quotation; otherwise, place them outside.

> The philosopher Brackenridge (16) asks, "How should we order our lives?"

but

Did Brackenridge (16) say that we might encounter "hostility from every quarter"?

Single quotation marks signal a quotation within a quotation.

Newspaper columnist George Will speaks of baseball's Hall of Fame as "a shrine to baseball's 'immortals'" (94). At the Hall of Fame, "The words describing a Babe Ruth exhibit speak of 'the might of his smite as he hit balls out of sight'" (94).

Indenting Long Quotations

Set off long prose quotations of four lines or more by indenting 1 inch, two clicks of the tab key, or ten spaces. Do not use quotation marks with the indented material. Place the parenthetical citation *after* the final mark of punctuation.

> According to the National Heritage Network, humans did not create the "web of life," but humans are responsible for conserving a biological diversity. The Network makes this observation:

> > In the web of life, all animals and plants are interconnected into a complex scheme of ecological communities. Each organism can be thought of as an individual web strand while ecological communities represent multiple strands. Biological diversity or biodiversity is essentially the scientific term that we apply to the web of life. ("Biodiversity")

> Because our future is inextricably bound to all other plants, animals, and resources, we are only harming ourselves when we bring harm to the diversity of the environment.

Citing Lines of Poetry

Incorporate short quotations of poetry (one or two lines) into your text. Use a slash with a space before and after to show line breaks.

> Part 3 of Eliot's "The Waste Land" (1922) remains a springtime search for nourishing water: "Sweet Thames, run softly, for I speak not loud or long" (line 176) says the speaker in "The Fire Sermon," while in Part 5 the speaker of

"What the Thunder Said" yearns for "a damp gust / Bringing rain" (lines 394–95).

Set off three or more lines of poetry by indenting 1 inch or by centering the lines.

Citing Drama

Indent the dialog of a play as a block. Begin with the character's name, indented 1 inch from the left margin and written in all capital letters. Follow the name with a period, tab forward, and begin the quotation. Start a new line when the dialog shifts to another character.

At the end of <u>Oedipus Rex</u>, Kreon chastises Oedipus, reminding him that he no longer has control over his own life nor that of his children.

> KREON.   Come now and leave your children.
> OEDIPUS.   No! Do not take them from me!
> KREON.   Think no longer
>   That you are in command here, but rather think
>   How, when you were, you served your own
>   destruction.

Changing Initial Capitals

In general, you should reproduce quoted materials exactly, yet one exception is permitted for logical reasons. Restrictive connectors, such as *that* and *because,* create restrictive clauses, which should not be set off by a comma.

> Another writer argues that "the single greatest impediment to our improving the lives of America's children is the myth that we are a child-oriented society" (Zigler 39).

Using Ellipsis Points to Omit Phrases

You may omit portions of quoted material with three spaced ellipsis points. In omitting material, do not change the meaning or take a quotation out of context.

Omission within a sentence. Three spaced ellipsis points (periods) signal omission from *within* a sentence:

> Phil Withim objects to the idea that "such episodes are intended to demonstrate that Vere . . . has the intelligence and insight to perceive the deeper issue" (118).

Omission at the end of a sentence.

Arnet and Jacques (10) declare that insects live in "all wild habitats as well as the full range of human environments. . . . "

Omission with a page citation at the end.

Arnet and Jacques declare that insects live in "all wild habitats as well as the full range of human environments . . . " (10).

Omission of complete sentences and paragraphs. This next example indicates the end of one sentence, the omission of one or more sentences, and a full sentence to end the passage.

Foreman reminds us that parents of teenagers must use expertise to "sidestep hassling over nonsense. . . . You can let some things slide because you know she'll learn, as you did, by trial and error" (10–11).

Omission of a line or lines of poetry.

Do ye hear the children weeping, O my brothers,
    Ere the sorrow comes with years?
They are leaning their young heads against their mothers,
    And <u>that</u> cannot stop their tears.
. . . .
They are weeping in the playtime of the others,
In the country of the free. (Browning 382)

Using Brackets to Alter Quotations

Alter a quotation if necessary to emphasize a point or to make something clear. Within brackets, add material, italicize an important word, or use the word *sic,* which notes an error in the original wording. Note the following examples.

This same critic indicates that "we must avoid the temptation to read it [<u>The Scarlet Letter</u>] heretically" (118).

"John F. Kennedy [was] an immortal figure of courage and dignity in the hearts of most Americans," notes one historian (Jones 82).

He says, for instance, that the "extended family is now rare in contemporary society, and with its demise the new parent has lost the *wisdom* [my emphasis] and daily support of

older, more experienced family members"
(Zigler 42).

Yearney says, "Theodore Roosevelt's final resting place in
Hyde Park, New York [sic], is a quiet and humble plot when
compared to his big game hunts in Africa or exploration in
the Brazilian jungle" (113).

Theodore Roosevelt is buried in Oyster Bay, New York; Franklin
D. Roosevelt is buried in Hyde Park, New York.

10c Writing the Works Cited References in MLA Style

The following lists explain with examples the correct reference
formats for books, periodicals, electronic sources, and other forms
of information.

Bibliography Form—Books

Author

Winchester, Simon. <u>Krakatoa</u>. New York: Harper, 2003.

Author, Anonymous

<u>The Song of Roland</u>. Trans. Glyn Burgess. New York:
Penguin, 1990.

Authors, Two or Three

Slywotzky, Adrian, Richard Wise, and Karl Weber. <u>How to
Grow When Markets Don't</u>. New York: Warner, 2003.

Authors, More Than Three

Use *et al.*, which means "and others," or list all the authors.

Clark, Duncan, et al. <u>Classical Music</u>. 3rd ed. New York:
Rough, 2001.

Senge, Peter, Nelda Cambron-McCabe, Timothy Lucas, Bryan
Smith, Janis Dutton, and Art Kleiner. <u>Schools That
Learn</u>. New York: Doubleday, 2000.

Author, Two or More Books by the Same Author

When an author has two or more works, do not repeat his or
her name with each entry. Rather, for the second and additional

entries, insert a continuous three-dash line flush with the left margin, followed by a period. Also, list the works alphabetically by the title (ignoring *a, an,* and *the*), not by the year of publication. In the following example, the *C* of *Chamber* precedes the *G* of *Goblet.*

> Rowling, J. K. <u>Harry Potter and the Chamber of Secrets</u>. New York: Scholastic, 1999.
>
> – – –. <u>Harry Potter and the Goblet of Fire</u>. New York: Scholastic, 2000.
>
> – – –. <u>Harry Potter and the Sorcerer's Stone</u>. New York: Scholastic, 1998.

Alphabetized Works, Encyclopedias, and Biographical Dictionaries

Well-known works need only the edition and the year of publication. If no author is listed, begin with the title of the article:

> Moran, Joseph. "Weather." <u>The World Book Encyclopedia</u>. 2003 ed.

If you cite a specific definition from among several, add *Def.* (Definition), followed by the appropriate number/letter of the definition.

> "Level." Def. 4a. <u>The American Heritage Dictionary of the English Language</u>. 4th ed. 2000.

Anthology, Component Part

Provide the inclusive page numbers for the piece, not just the page or pages you cited in the text.

> Reagon, Bernice. "Black Music in Our Hands." <u>The Conscious Reader</u>. Eds. Caroline Shrodes, Harry Finestone, and Michael Shugrue. 8th ed. Boston: Allyn, 2001. 345–49.

The Bible

Do not underscore or italicize the word Bible or the books of the Bible. Common editions need no publication information, but do underscore or italicize the titles of special editions.

> The Bible. [Denotes King James version]
>
> The Bible. The Old Testament. CD-ROM. Audio Bible, 2003.
>
> <u>NIV [New International Version] Study Bible</u>. Personal Size Revised Edition. N.p.: Zondervan, 2002.

Cross-References to Works in a Collection

Cite several selections from one anthology by giving a full reference to the anthology and abbreviated cross-references to the individual selections.

> Elbow, Peter, and Pat Belanoff. <u>Being a Writer</u>. Boston:
> McGraw, 2003.
>
> Koo, Eunsook. "Exploring the Writing Process." Elbow and
> Belanoff 181.
>
> Spencer, Beth. "The Act of Writing as Prayer." Elbow and
> Belanoff 126–28.
>
> Wilbur, Richard. "The Writer." Elbow and Belanoff 220.

Edition

Cite any edition beyond the first.

> Acredolo, Linda P., Susan Goodwyn, and Douglas Abrams.
> <u>Baby Signs</u>. Rev. ed. Boston: McGraw, 2002.

Editor, Translator, Illustrator, or Compiler

List the editor first only if your in-text citation refers to the work of the editor (for example, the editor's introduction or notes, as in "Toibin iii" or "Toibin n. 17.").

> Toibin, Colm, ed. <u>Irish Fiction</u>. London: Penguin, 1999.

Sourcebooks and Casebooks

> Elbow, Peter, and Pat Belanoff. "Reflecting on Your Writing."
> <u>Being a Writer: A Community of Writers Revisited</u>.
> Boston: McGraw, 2003. 329–50.

Title of a Book in Another Language

In general, use lowercase letters for foreign titles and subtitles except for the first word and proper names. Provide a translation in brackets if you think it necessary (e.g., Étranger [The Stranger] or Praha [Prague]).

> Eco, Umberto. <u>El nombre de la rosa</u>. New York: Sites, 2000.

Volume

> Borgese, Elisabeth Mann. <u>Ocean Yearbook</u>. Vol. 17. Chicago:
> U of Chicago P, 2003.

Bibliography Form—Periodicals

Author

Feldman, Stanley. "Enforcing Social Conformity: A Theory of Authoritarianism." <u>Political Psychology</u> 24.1 (March 2003): 41–74.

Author, Anonymous

"British Muslims: R.I.P. for Recruitment to Jihad." <u>The Week</u> 16 (May 2003): 15.

Interview, Published

Vonnegut, Kurt. Interview with David Hoppe. "Still Vonnegut." <u>Utne Reader</u> (June 2003): 86–89.

Journal, with All Issues for a Year Paged Continuously

Bartley, William. "Imagining the Future in <u>The Awakening</u>." <u>College English</u> 62 (2000): 719–46.

Journal, Each Issue Paged Anew

Add the issue number after the volume number and/or add the month.

Dawisha, Adeed, and Karen Dawisha. "How to Build a Democratic Iraq." <u>Foreign Affairs</u> 82.3 (May/June 2003): 36–50.

Loose-leaf Collection

If the article appears in an information service with several articles on a common topic, use this next form:

Cox, Rachel S. "Protecting the National Parks." <u>CQ Researcher</u> 16 July 2000: 523+. <u>The Environment</u>. Washington, DC: Congressional Quarterly, 2000. No. 23.

If the service reprints articles from other sources, use this next form, which shows original publication data and then information on the SIRS booklet—title, editor, and volume number.

Hodge, Paul. "The Andromeda Galaxy." <u>Mercury</u> July/Aug. 1993: 98+. <u>Physical Science</u>. Ed. Eleanor Goldstein. Vol. 2. Boca Raton: SIRS, 1994. Art. 24.

Magazine

Provide an exact date. Do not list the volume and issue numbers.

Walsh, Kenneth T. "Air Force One." <u>U.S. News & World
Report</u> 19 May 2003: 26–35.

Supply inclusive page numbers (202–09, 85–115, or 1,112–24), but if an article is paged here and there throughout the issue (for example, pages 74, 78, and 81–88), write only the first page number and a plus sign with no intervening space:

Sim, Jillian. "Monroe Trotter: Profile in Protest." <u>American
Legacy</u> Summer 2003: 73+.

Notes, Editorials, Queries, Reports, Comments, Letters

Identify the type of pieces that are not full-fledged articles.

Trainor, Jennifer Seibel, and Deborah Klein. Comment and
Response. <u>College English</u> 62 (2000): 767–72.
Maltby, Richard E., Jr. "Save One for Me." Puzzle. <u>Harper's</u>
June 2003: 87.

Review Article

Name the reviewer and the title of the review. Then write *Rev.
of* and the title of the work being reviewed, followed by a comma, and the name of the author or producer.

Grant, Angelynn. "Differentiate or Die." Rev. of <u>Differentiate
or Die</u>, by Jack Trout. <u>Communication Arts</u> 45.2
(May/June 2003): 140+.

Title, Quotation Marks within the Article's Title

Gatta, John J. "The Scarlet Letter as Pre-text for Flannery
O'Connor's 'Good Country People.' " <u>Nathaniel
Hawthorne Review</u> 16 (1990): 6–9.

Title of a Book within the Article's Title

Cornils, Ingo. "The Martians Are Coming! War, Peace, Love,
and Scientific Progress in H. G. Wells's <u>The War of the
Worlds</u> and Kurd Labwitz's <u>Auf Zwei Planeten</u>."
<u>Comparative Literature</u> 55.1 (Winter 2003): 24–41.

Bibliography Form—Newspapers

Provide the name of the author; the title of the article; the name of the newspaper as it appears on the masthead, omitting any introductory article (e.g., <u>Wall Street Journal</u>, not <u>The Wall Street Journal</u>); and the complete date—day, month (abbreviated), and year. Omit volume and issue numbers. Provide a page number as listed (e.g., 21, B–6, 14C, D3).

Newspaper in One Section

Reedy, Justin. "Axle Grease and Guitar Strings." <u>Clayton News Daily</u> 30 May 2003: 1+.

Newspaper with Lettered Sections

Maxwell, John. "Learn, Grow, and Succeed through Mistakes." <u>Atlanta Business Chronicle</u> 30 May 2003: 3A.

Newspaper with Numbered Sections

Jones, Tim. "New Media May Excite, While Old Media Attract." <u>Chicago Tribune</u> 28 July 1997, sec. 4: 2.

Newspaper Column, Cartoon, Comic Strip, Advertisement, Etc.

Add a description to explain the special nature of the source.

Donlan, Thomas G. "Fine Tuning." Column. <u>Barron's</u> 26 May 2003: 31.

Bibliography Form—Government Documents

As a general rule, place information in the bibliographic entry in this order: government body or agency, subsidiary body, title of document, identifying numbers, publication facts. When you cite two or more works by the same government, substitute three hyphens for the name of each government or body you repeat:

United States. Cong. House.

– – –. – – –. Senate.

– – –. Dept. of Justice.

Begin with the author's name, if known, especially if you cited it in the text.

Tully, Jane. "Responding to Terrorism: Recovery, Resilience, Readiness." Substance Abuse and Mental Health Service Administration. Department of Health and Human Services. <u>SAMHSA NEWS.</u> 10 (2002): 1. Doc. 20.245.10/1. Washington: GPO, 2002.

Congressional Papers

> United States. Cong. Senate. Subcommittee on Juvenile Justice
>   of the Committee on the Judiciary. <u>Juvenile Justice: A</u>
>   <u>New Focus on Prevention</u>. 102nd Cong., 2nd sess. S.
>   Hearing 102–1045. Washington, DC: GPO, 1992.

If you provide a citation to the *Congressional Record,* you should abbreviate it and provide only the date and page numbers.

> <u>Cong. Rec</u>. 23 May 2003: S7101–05.

Executive Branch Documents

> United States. Dept. of State. <u>Foreign Relations of the United</u>
>   <u>States: Diplomatic Papers, 1943</u>. 5 vols. Washington:
>   GPO, 1943–44.
> – – –. President. <u>2003 Economic Report of the President</u>.
>   Washington: GPO, 2003.

Documents of State Governments

Publication information on state papers varies. The goal of your documentation is to provide sufficient data for your reader to find the document.

> <u>Tennessee Election Returns, 1796–1825</u>. Microfilm.
>   Nashville: Tennessee State Library and Archives, n.d.:
>   M-Film JK 5292 T46.

Legal Citations and Public Statutes

> California. Constitution. Art. 2, sec. 4.
> Environmental Protection Agency et al. v. Mink et al.
> US Reports, CDX. 1972.
> 15 US Code. Sec. 78h. 1964.

Bibliography Form—Electronic Sources (Internet, E-mail, Databases)

Abstract

> Riso, Lawrence P., et al. "Cognitive Aspects of Chronic
>   Depression." <u>Journal of Abnormal Psychology</u> 112
>   (2003). Abstract. 10 May 2003 <http:www.apa.org/
>   journals/abn/0203ab.htm/#7>.

Anonymous Article

"Child Passenger Safety." <u>National Highway Traffic</u>
   <u>Safety Administration</u>. n.d. 11 Sept. 2003
   <http://www.nhtsa.dot.gov/people/injury/childps/>.

Archive or Scholarly Project

Coleridge, Samuel Taylor. "Kubla Khan." <u>The Samuel Taylor</u>
   <u>Coleridge Archive</u>. Ed. Marjorie A. Tiefert. 10 May
   1999. U of Virginia Lib. 18 Aug. 2003 <http://
   etext.lib.virginia.edu/stc/Coleridge/poems/
   Kubla_Khan.html>.

Article Reproduced from a Scholarly Journal

Fillmore, K. M., W. C. Kerr, and A. Bostrom. "Changes in
   Drinking Status, Serious Illness and Mortality."
   <u>Journal of Studies on Alcohol</u> 64 (2003): 278–85. 22
   Sept. 2003 <http://www.rci.rutgers.edu/~cas2/
   journal/march03/>.

Chapter or Portion of a Book

Place the chapter title after the author's name:

Dewey, John. "Waste in Education." <u>The School and Society</u>.
   Chicago: U of Chicago P, 1907. 4 Feb. 2003 <http://
   spartan.ac.brocku.ca/~lward/dewey/Dewey_1907/
   Dewey_1907c.html>.

E-mail

Grissom, Ellen. "Writing Criteria." E-mail to the author. 19
   Jan. 2004.

Encyclopedia Article Online

"Coleridge, Samuel Taylor." <u>Encyclopedia Britannica Online</u>.
   Vers. 99.1. 1994–99. Encyclopedia Britannica. 19 Aug.
   2003 <http://www.eb.com/bol/topic?eu=25136&sctn=1>.

Film, Video, or Film Clip Online

"Transfiguration of the Cross." <u>The History of the Orthodox</u>
   <u>Christian Church</u>. 2003. GoTelecom Online. 24 Oct.

2003 <http://www.goarch.org/en/multimedia/video/ #transfiguration>.

Web Site

Robert Penn Warren: 1905–1989. 15 Jan. 2004 <http:// www.english.uiuc.edu/maps/poets/s_z/warren/ warren.htm>.

Magazine Article Online

Koretz, Gene. "Out of Work, Out of the Loop." BusinessWeek Online 15 May 2003. 2 Oct. 2003 <http://asia.businessweek.com/careers/content/may2003/ ca20030515_2074_ca004.htm>.

Online Forum or Discussion

Kalb, Jim. "Conservatism FAQ." Online Posting. 1 June 2003. Environment Newsgroup. 11 Feb. 2004 <http://nwww.faqs.org/faqs/conservatism/faq/>.

Newspaper Article, Column, or Editorial Online

Prater, Connie. "Small Study Offers Big Hope for Diabetics." Miami Herald 2 June 2003. 2 June 2003 <http:// www.miami.com/mld/miamiherald/living/5999174.htm>.

Sound Clip or Recording

Keillor, Garrison. "Writer and Radio Personality Garrison Keillor." Fresh Air Audio. NPR Online. 18 Oct. 2002. Audio transcript. 22 Apr. 2003 <http://discover.npr.org/ features/feature.jhtml?wfId=1151873>.

University Posting, Online Article

Chambers, Aaron. "Pedophiles to Pornographers." Online Posting. May 2003. U of Illinois at Springfield. 28 July 2003 <http://illinoisissues.uis.edu/features/2003may/ offender.html>.

Bibliography Form—Databases
Article at a Library's Online Service with a Listed URL

Most libraries have converted their computer searches to online databases, such as Lexis-Nexis, ProQuest Direct, EBSCOhost, Electric

Library, InfoTrac, and others. If the source provides the URL, omit the identifying numbers for the database or the keyword used in the search and include the URL. Here's an example from InfoTrac:

> Lee, Catherine C. "The South in Toni Morrison's 'Song of Solomon': Initiation, Healing, and Home." <u>Studies in the Literary Imagination</u> 31 (1998): 109–23. Abstract. InfoTrac. U of Tennessee, Hodges Lib. 19 Sept. 2003 <http://firstsearch.oclc.org/next=NEXTCMD>.

Article with Only a Starting Page Number of the Original Print Version

> Worthen, W. B. "Recent Studies in Tudor and Stuart Drama." Review. <u>Studies in English Literature, 1500–1900</u> 42 (2002): 399– . 11 March 2004 <http://www.yalegroup.com/>.

Note: Leave a space after the hyphen and before the period.

Article from an Online Service to Which You Personally Subscribe

Many students research topics from their homes, where they use such services as America Online or Netscape. If the URL is provided, use the form of this next example.

> "Nutrition and Cancer." <u>Discovery Health</u> 1 May 2000. 30 Sept. 2003 <http://www.discoveryhealth.com/Sc000/8096/164609.html>.

Article from an Online Service with an Unlisted or Scrambled URL

Two possible forms are available to you when the online service provides no URL.

1. *Keyword.* If you access the site by using a keyword, provide a citation that gives the name of the service, the date of access, and the keyword:

> Esslin, Martin. "Theater of the Absurd." <u>Grolier Multimedia Encyclopedia</u>. 1995 ed. Netscape. 22 Aug. 2003. Keyword: Theater of the Absurd.

2. *Path.* If you follow a series of topic labels to reach the article, and no URL is provided, write the word *Path* followed by the

sequence of topic labels you followed to obtain the article. Use a semicolon to separate each topic.

"Kate Chopin: A Re-Awakening." 23 June 1999. <u>PBS. College Webivore</u>. Netscape. 24 Jan. 2004. Path: US Literature; 19th Century; Women Authors; Chopin, Kate (1850–1904).

CD-ROM Sources

Cite this type of source as you would a book, and then provide information to the electronic source you accessed. Conform to the examples that follow:

"Abolitionist Movement." <u>Compton's Interactive Encyclopedia</u>. CD-ROM. The Learning Company, 1999.

The Bible. The Old Testament. CD-ROM. Parsippany, NJ: Bureau Development, 1999.

English Poetry Full-Text Database. CD-ROM. Cambridge, UK: Chadwyck, 1993.

"John F. Kennedy." InfoPedia. CD-ROM. N.p.: Future Vision, n.d.

Bibliography Form—Artistic Works and Performances

Artwork

"Elie Nadelman: Sculptor of Modern Life." Whitney Museum of American Art, New York. 4 June 2003.

Use this next form to cite reproductions in books and journals.

Raphael. "School of Athens." The Vatican, Rome. <u>The World Book Encyclopedia</u>. 2003 ed.

Broadcast Interview

Gray, Jim. "NBA Coaching Vacancies." Interview. ESPN. 4 June 2003.

Film, Videocassette, or DVD

Cite the title of a film, the director, the distributor, and the year.

<u>Ice Age</u>. Dir. Chris Wedge. Screenplay by Michael J. Wilson. 20th Century Fox, 2002.

<u>Citizen Kane</u>. Dir. Orson Welles. 1941. DVD. Warner, 2002.

Crimmins, Morton. "Robert Lowell: American Poet." Lecture.
Videocassette. Western State U, 2003.

Performance

Treat a performance (e.g., play, opera, ballet, or concert) as you would a film, but include the site (normally the theater and city) and the date of the performance.

Buchbinder, Rudolph. "Gershwin Piano Concerto in F." New
York Philharmonic. Avery Fisher Hall, New York. 5
June 2003.

Lakota Sioux Indian Dance Theatre. Cherokee Heritage
Center, Tahlequah, OK. 12 May 2002.

Public Address or Lecture

Identify the speaker and the nature of the address (e.g., Lecture, Reading); include the location (normally the lecture hall and city) and the date of the performance.

Darrish, Murray B. "Documenting an Early Missouri
Family." Lecture. St. Louis Genealogical Soc., St. Louis.
9 Sept. 2003.

Recording on Record, Tape, or Disk

Indicate the medium (e.g., audiocassette, audiotape [reel-to-reel tape], CD, or LP [long-playing record]).

"Chaucer: The Nun's Priest's Tale." <u>Canterbury Tales</u>. Narr. in
Middle English by Alex Edmonds. Audiocassette.
London, 2003.

Television or Radio Program

<u>The Way We Live Now</u>. By Anthony Trollope. Adapt. Andrew
Davies. Dir. David Yates. Perf. David Suchet, Matthew
Macfayden, Paloma Baeza, and Cheryl Campbell. 4
episodes. <u>Masterpiece Theatre</u>. Introd. Russell Baker.
PBS. WCDN, Nashville. 1 June 2003.

Bibliography Form—Other Sources

When you have an unusual source, label it in the bibliography entry with such words as *advertisement, letter, map, transparency,* or *voice mail.* Here are a few examples of this form.

Schuler, Wren. "Prufrock and His Cat." Unpublished essay, 2003.

Alphabet. Chart. Columbus: Scholastic, 2003.

Shore, Zandra Lesley. "Girls Reading Culture: Autobiography as Inquiry into Teaching the Body, the Romance, and the Economy of Love." Diss. U of Toronto, 1999.

Tuckerman, H. T. "James Fenimore Cooper." Microfilm. <u>North American Review</u> 89 (1859): 298–316.

10d Formatting the Paper in MLA Style

The format of a research paper consists of the following parts (items 1, 3, and 6 are required):

1. Opening page with title
2. Outline (if required)
3. The text of the paper
4. Content notes
5. Appendix
6. Works Cited

Title Page or Opening Page

A research paper in MLA style does not require a separate title page. See page 141 for an example.

Outline

Include your outline with the finished manuscript only if your instructor requires it.

The Text of the Paper

Double-space throughout the entire paper. In general, you should *not* use subtitles or numbered divisions for your paper, even if it becomes twenty pages long. Do not start Notes or Works Cited on the final page of text.

Content Endnotes Page

Label this page with the word *Notes* centered at the top edge of the sheet. Number the notes in sequence. Double-space all entries and double-space between them.

Appendix

Place additional material, if necessary, in an appendix that precedes the Works Cited page. This is the logical location for tables and illustrations, computer data, questionnaire results, complicated statistics, mathematical proofs, and detailed descriptions of special equipment.

Works Cited

Center the heading *Works Cited* 1 inch from the top edge of the sheet. Continue the page-numbering sequence in the upper right corner. Double-space throughout. Use the hanging indention—that is, set the first line of each entry flush left and indent subsequent lines five spaces or 1/2 inch. Alphabetize by the last name of the author. See page 147 for an example.

10e   Writing a Literary Paper in MLA Style

Sample Research Paper

A sample research paper by Melinda Mosier is reproduced in the pages that follow. Annotations in the margins explain elements of style that may be important in the development of your paper.

Mosier 1

Melinda Mosier
Professor Thompson
Humanities 1020
6 April 2003

Listening to Hamlet: The Soliloquies

A soliloquy is a dramatic form of discourse in which a person reveals inner thoughts and feelings while alone on stage or while unaware that others might be within the range of their voice. But then, the person might also deliver such a speech while knowing full well that somebody is listening. Thus, the dramatic convention has complications, and when Shakespeare uses it with a complex character like Hamlet, it appears in a variety of forms. Critical authorities have agreed that the soliloquies reveal the inner

Mosier opens with a definition.

Mosier 2

feelings of Hamlet (Auden, Bloom, and Wilson), and they

disagree somewhat in their interpretations. This study, however, will examine the settings within which the soliloquies occur and interpret the direction of Hamlet's remarks—inward to himself and outward to a perceived listener.

The first soliloquy occurs in Act 1, scene 2, lines 133–64, immediately after King Claudius and Queen Gertrude have left in a flourish. His mother has just admonished Hamlet for wearing black after these many days following the death of his father, and he has responded with a play on the word *seems,* indicating in lines 79–89, that his mourning clothes are "but the trappings and the suits of woe," but that he has within a mournful spirit that is so deep it "passes show." He is stricken to his core by sadness. Then he is left alone and cries out:

> Oh, that this too too sullied flesh would melt,
> Thaw, and resolve itself into a dew,
> Or that the Everlasting had not fixed
> His canon 'gainst self-slaughter. O God, God,
> How weary, stale, flat and unprofitable
> Seem to me all the uses of this world! (1.2.133–38)[1]

This opening gives its obvious nod toward suicide and to the inner darkness of his soul, which even black clothing cannot show in full force. But Shakespeare uses this soliloquy for another important purpose—the son's verbal attack on his mother, Gertrude. She has just left in a flourish with the king, her new husband. Hamlet reveals his disgust with her because she has moved with "most wicked speed" (1.2.161) to marry Claudius, her dead husband's brother. Hamlet sees the union as an act of

---

[1]Quotations from the text come from the Folger Library edition.

Mosier 3

incest and closes the soliloquy by saying: "It is not, nor it
cannot come to good: / But break, my heart, for I must hold
my tongue!" (1.2.163–64). Some critics, like Ernest Jones,
would suggest that Hamlet is jealous of Claudius for
winning a love that he (Hamlet) wanted, but that idea
is severely weakened by Hamlet's damning words
against her dexterity within *"incestuous sheets"*
(my emphasis).

> **Two lines of the play can be quoted in the text, with the lines separated by a slash.**

The second soliloquy occurs in Act 2.2.576–634. The
setting again has great relevance to Hamlet's words. An
actor has just described how his company would portray
the anguished and agonized cries of Hecuba, who must
watch as her husband, Priam, the king of Troy, is hacked to
death. Now, Hamlet is dismayed because a mere actor can
show such passion in a fictional portrayal:

> **This section demonstrates the manner in which Mosier interprets one of the soliloquies, citing from it and explaining the implications in light of the play's setting.**

> O, what a rogue and peasant slave am I!
> Is it not monstrous that this player here,
> But in a fiction, in a dream of passion,
> Could force his soul so to his own conceit
> That from her working all his visage wanned,
> Tears in his eyes, distraction in his aspect,
> A broken voice, and his whole function suiting
> With forms to his conceit? And all for nothing!
> For Hecuba!
> What's Hecuba to him, or he to Hecuba,
> That he should weep for her? (2.2.576–86)

Comparing himself with the actor, Hamlet calls himself
a "dull and muddy-mettled rascal" who "can say nothing;
no, not for a king, / Upon whose property and most dear
life / A damn'd defeat was made. Am I a coward?"
(2.2.594–98). Hamlet is tortured in regard to his mother,
who is his version of Hecuba (70). Next, Shakespeare uses
the soliloquy to set out another comparison—one between a

Mosier 4

"pigeon-livered" (2.2.604) Prince Hamlet and an active and crafty Prince Hamlet. He recognizes his failure:

> Why, what an ass am I! This is most brave,
> That I, the son of a dear father murdered,
> Prompted to my revenge by heaven and hell,
> Must, like a whore, unpack my heart with words
> And fall a-cursing, like a very drab,
> A scullion!
> Fie upon 't! (2.2.611–16)

But suddenly, Hamlet changes his attitude, saying, "About, my brain!" This means, get busy, brain, and go to work! So now he plots the play within a play, saying, "The play's the thing / Wherein I'll catch the conscience of the king" (2.2.633–34).

In short, this soliloquy has three parts, all tied to the setting—praise for a performer who can act with passion, disgust with himself for his failure to act, and then his cunning plan for tricking the king by using the actors.

Later, we see Hamlet still motivating himself, and again Shakespeare uses a comparison to force the issue—a prince of Norway versus the prince of Denmark. The setting is a plain in Denmark where Fortinbras, the nephew of the Norwegian king, leads an army across Denmark to attack a small section of Poland, fortified by 20,000 soldiers, but in truth the piece of land is not of great value. The Norwegian Captain explains, "We go to gain a little patch of ground / That hath in it no profit but the name. / To pay five ducats, five, I would not farm it . . . " (4.4.19–21). Hamlet recognizes the irony in the contrast—Fortinbras brazenly fights for what he deems his even though it has little value but Hamlet refuses to fight in revenge for the very real death of his father.

> How stand I then,
> That have a father killed, a mother stained,

Mosier 5

Excitements of my reason and my blood,

    And let all sleep. . . . (4.4.59–68)

The Norwegians will fight and die for a worthless cause while he procrastinates. "O, from this time forth," he cries, "My thoughts be bloody, or be nothing worth!" (4.4.69–70).

Thus, Shakespeare has carefully crafted a setting for each soliloquy, and the device of <u>comparison</u> plays a key role. In the first, Hamlet cries out that his soul is darker even than the black funeral garb he wears because of his mother's incestuous behavior. In the second, his behavior seems impotent (and perhaps that's a valid term) in comparison with the actor who cries so passionately for Hecuba, a distant historic figure far removed from Hamlet's recent loss of a father. In the third, he compares and contrasts the magnetism of death against "the dread of something after death, / The undiscovered country, from whose bourn / No traveler returns . . . " (3.1.86–87). In the fourth soliloquy, he reminds himself that he cannot perform cruel, unnatural acts like Nero. In the fifth, he stands ashamed of his inactivity in comparison to an aggressive Norwegian prince.

Mosier reviews briefly the soliloquies to show how Hamlet compares himself to someone else.

In every instance Hamlet compares himself to someone else—a white knight; a passionate actor; a vibrant, throbbing human being; a Nero figure; or an aggressive soldier. Perhaps W. H. Auden expresses it best:

Hamlet lacks faith in God and in himself. Consequently he must define his existence in terms of others, e.g., I am the man whose mother married his uncle who murdered his father. He would like to become what the Greek tragic hero is, a creature of situation. Hence his inability to act, for he can only "act," i.e., play at possibilities. He is fundamentally <u>bored</u>, and for that reason he acts theatrically. (164)

Mosier 6

Shakespeare leaves Hamlet alone on stage in the soliloquies to "act out" his anguish because he could not act otherwise. Each setting for each soliloquy was a pivotal but stifling moment. If we have only the soliloquies before us, we can see that Hamlet will fail and "prophesy the election lights / on Fortinbras" (5.2.392–93), the man of action, not a man of "acting."

Mosier 7

Bibliography

Auden, W. H. <u>Lectures on Shakespeare</u>. Ed. Arthur
    Kirsch. Princeton: Princeton UP, 2000.

Bloom, Harold. <u>Hamlet: Poem Unlimited</u>. New York:
    Riverhead-Penguin, 2003.

Cannon, Charles K. "'As in a Theater'": <u>Hamlet</u> in the
    Light of Calvin's Doctrine of Predestination." <u>Studies
    in English Literature, 1500–1600</u> 11 (1971: 203–22.
    <u>JSTOR</u>. 8 Apr. 2003 <http://www.jstor.org/search>.

Goethe, Johann Wolfgang. "A Soul Unfit." <u>Wilhelm
    Meister's Apprenticeship</u>. Trans. Thomas Carlyle.
    <u>Hamlet: A Norton Critical Edition</u>. Ed. Cyrus Hoy.
    2nd ed. New York: Norton, 1992.

Jones, Ernest. "The Oedipus-Complex as an Explanation
    of Hamlet's Mystery: A Study in Motive." <u>American
    Journal of Psychology</u> 21.1 (1910): 72–113.
    <u>Shakespeare Navigators</u>. 8 Apr. 2003
    <http://www.clicknotes.com/jones>.

Shakespeare, William. <u>The Tragedy of Hamlet, Prince of
    Denmark</u>. <u>The New Folger Library Shakespeare</u>. Ed.
    Barbara A. Mowat and Paul Werstine. New York:
    Washington Square P, 1992.

Wilson, Dover. <u>What Happens in Hamlet</u>. 1935.
    Cambridge, UK: Cambridge UP, 2001.

Youngson, Robert M. <u>The Madness of Hamlet and Other
    Extraordinary States of Mind</u>. New York: Carroll &
    Graf, 1999.

Form for a book.

Citation to a Web site.

A citation to a database's search page.

Citation to the edition used and cited in the paper.

11

Writing in APA Style

You may need to write the research paper in a style that features the authority's name and the year of publication.

11a Meeting the Demands of the Assignment

In the social sciences, your assignment is likely to be a:

- Theoretical article
- Report of empirical research
- Review article

Writing Theoretical Articles

A theory paper usually asks you to draw on existing research to trace the development of a theory or to compare theories. Your theoretical analysis will examine the current thinking about a social topic such as criminal behavior, dysfunctional families, and learning disorders. The theory paper generally accomplishes four things:

1. Identifies a problem or hypothesis with historical implications in the scientific community.
2. Traces the development and history of the evolution of a related theory.
3. Systematically analyzes the articles that have explored the problem.
4. Arrives at a judgment and discussion of the prevailing theory.

Reporting on Empirical Research

When you conduct original research in the field or lab, you should write a report that details your procedures and findings. Beforehand, you may also write a proposal to explain your hypothesis and the manner in which you will conduct the study. See pages

52-54 for the discussion of observation, testing, and other methods for conducting the research. Typically, an empirical study:

1. Introduces the problem or hypothesis under investigation and explains the purpose of the work.
2. Describes the design and methodology of the research.
3. Reports the results of the investigation or test.
4. Discusses, interprets, and explores the implications of the findings.

Reviewing Articles and Books

A common assignment is to write a critical evaluation of a published article or book, or of a set of articles on a common topic. The purpose of the paper is to examine the state of current research. The paper serves several purposes:

1. Defines the problem to clarify the hypothesis.
2. Summarizes the article(s) or book under review.
3. Analyzes the literature to discover strengths, weaknesses, and inconsistencies in the research.
4. Recommends additional research that might grow logically from the work under review.

(See pages 95-102 for an example of a review of literature.)

11b Establishing a Critical Approach

In scientific writing, the thesis statement (see pages 8-11) usually appears as a hypothesis, statement of principle, or an enthymeme.

The *hypothesis* is a theory requiring testing and analysis, which you do during your research. It is an idea expressed as a truth for the purpose of argument and investigation and testing. Put another way, it makes a prediction based on a theory.

> It was predicted that patients who suffer a compulsive
> bulimia disorder would have a more disrupted family life.

In similar fashion, the *statement of principle* makes a declarative statement in defense of an underlying but unstated theory. This type of report attempts to prove a hypothetical principle on the basis of testing, observation, interviews, and other methods of field research as explained on pages 46-54.

> The most effective recall cue is the one encoded within the
> event to be remembered.

11c Writing in the Proper Tense for an APA-styled Paper

APA style requires that you use the past tense or the present perfect tense ("Marshall *stipulated*" or "the work of Elmford and Mills *has demonstrated*"). APA style does require present tense when you discuss the results of your research (e.g., *the results confirm* or *the study indicates*) and when you mention established knowledge (e.g., *the therapy offers some hope* or *salt contributes to hypertension*).

11d Blending Sources into Your Writing

APA style uses these conventions for in-text citations:

- Last names only
- The year, within parentheses, immediately after the name of the author
- Page numbers with a direct quotation, seldom with a paraphrase
- Use of *p.* or *pp.* before page numbers

Montague (2004) advanced the idea of combining the social sciences and mathematics to chart human behavior.

One study advanced the idea of combining the social sciences and mathematics to chart human behavior (Montague 2004).

Montague (2004) has advanced the idea of "soft mathematics," which is the practice of "applying mathematics to study people's behavior" (p. B4).

Citing a Block of Material

Present a quotation of forty words or more as a separate block, indented five spaces or 1/2 inch from the left margin. Do not enclose it with quotation marks. Set parenthetical citations outside the last period.

> Albert (2003) reported the following:
>
> Whenever these pathogenic organisms attack the human body and begin to multiply, the infection is set in motion. The host responds to this parasitic invasion with efforts to cleanse itself of the invading agents. When rejection efforts of the host become

visible (fever, sneezing, congestion), the disease status exists. (pp. 314–315)

Citing a Work with More Than One Author

When one work has two or more authors, use *and* in the text but *&* in the parenthetical citation.

Werner and Throckmorton (2003) offered statistics on the toxic levels of water samples from six rivers.

It was reported (Werner & Throckmorton, 2003) that toxic levels exceeded the maximum allowed each year since 1983.

For three to five authors, name them all in the first entry (e.g., Torgerson, Andrews, Smith, Lawrence, & Dunlap, 2003), but thereafter use *et al.* (e.g., Torgerson et al., 2003). For six or more authors, employ *et al.* in the first and in all subsequent instances (e.g., Fredericks et al., 2003).

Citing More Than One Work by an Author

Use small letters (a, b, c) to identify two or more works published in the same year by the same author:

Horton (2002; cf. Thomas, 1999a, p. 89, and 1999b, p. 426) suggested an intercorrelation of these testing devices. But after multiple-group analysis, Welston (2004, esp. p. 211) reached an opposite conclusion.

Citing Indirect Sources

Use a double reference to cite somebody who has been quoted in a book or article:

In other research, Massie and Rosenthal (2003) studied home movies of children diagnosed with autism, but determining criteria was difficult due to the differences in quality and dating of the available videotapes (cited in Osterling & Dawson, 2004, p. 248).

Citing an Anonymous Author

When no author is listed for a work, cite the title:

The cost per individual student has continued to rise rapidly ("Money Concerns," 2004, p. 2).

Citing Electronic Sources

In general, omit page numbers for articles you find on the Internet. However, if an online article shows original numbering, by all means supply that information in your citation: (Jones, 2004, par. 5).

> The most common type of diabetes is non-insulin-dependent diabetes mellitus (NIDDM), which "affects 90% of those with diabetes and usually appears after age 40" (Larson, 1996, par. 3).

Web Site

> The Web site Thomas (1997) has provided the four-page outline to the *Superfund Cleanup Acceleration Act of 1997*, which will provoke community participation, enforce remedial actions, establish liability, and protect natural resources.

Abstract

> "Psychologically oriented techniques used to elicit confessions may undermine their validity" (Kassin, 1997, abstract).

Online Magazine

> *BusinessWeek Online* (2001) reported that Napster's idea of peer-to-peer computing is a precursor to new Web applications, even though the courts might close them down.

E-mail

Personal communications, which others cannot retrieve, should be cited in the text only and not mentioned at all in the bibliography.

CD, DVD, Individual Disks

> *Compton's Interactive Encyclopedia* (1999) has explained that the Abolition Society, which originated in England in 1787, appears to be the first organized group in opposition to slavery. Later, in 1823, the Anti-Slavery Society was formed by Thomas Fowell Buxton, who wielded power as a member of Parliament.

11e   Preparing the List of References

Use the title *References* for your bibliography page. Alphabetize the entries and double-space throughout. Every reference used in your text, except personal communications, should appear in your alphabetical list of references at the end of the paper. Use the hanging indent—that is, set the first line of each entry flush left and indent succeeding lines five spaces. Italicize or underline names of books, periodicals, and volume numbers, including associated punctuation marks.

Bibliography Form—Books

Turlington, C. (2003). *Living yoga: Creating a life practice.* New York: Hyperion.

List chronologically, not alphabetically, two or more works by the same author; for example, Fitzgerald's 2002 publication would precede her 2003 publication.

Part of a Book

List author(s), date, chapter or section title, editor (with name in normal order) preceded by *In* and followed by *(Ed.)* or *(Eds.),* the name of the book (underscored or italicized), page numbers of the cited section of the book (in parentheses), place of publication, and publisher.

Graham, K. (2003). The male bashing stereotype. In P. Elbow & P. Belanoff (Eds.), *Being a writer* (pp. 249–254). New York: McGraw Hill.

Encyclopedia or Dictionary

To cite the entire work, use this form:

Eatwell, J., Milgate, M., & Newman, P. (Eds.) (1998). *New Palgrave: A dictionary of economics* (Rev. ed., Vols. 1–4). London: Macmillan.

To cite a specific entry, use this form:

Moran, J. (2002). Weather. In *World book encyclopedia* (Vol. 21, pp. 201–209). Chicago: Field Enterprises.

Bibliography Form—Periodicals
Article in a Journal

Smiler, A. P., Gagne, D. D., & Stine-Morrow, E. A. L. (2003). Aging, memory load, and resource allocation during reading. *Psychology and Aging, 18,* 203–209.

Article Retrieved from a Server

Wakschlag, L. S., & Leventhal, B. L. (1996). Consultation with young autistic children and their families. *Journal of the American Academy of Child and*

Adolescent Psychiatry, 35, 963–65. Retrieved August 8, 2004, from Expanded Academic Index database.

Article in a Magazine

Harman, T. D. (2003, August). The unchanging plan. *Civil War Times, 32,* 43–47.

Creedon, Jeremiah. (2003, May/June). The greening of Tony Soprano. *Utne,* pp. 73–77.

Note: Show the volume number if it is readily available; without a volume number, use *pp.* with the page numbers.

Article in a Newspaper

Haynes, T. (2003, June 10). Saving the Columbia. *Boston Globe,* p. C12.

Abstract as the Cited Source

Pannewitz, S., Schlensog, M., Green, T. G. A., Sancho, L. G., & Schroeter, B. (2003). Are lichens active under snow in continental Antarctica? [Abstract]. *Oecologia, 135,* 30–38.

Gandhi, J. (2003). Political institutions under dictatorship [Abstract]. Unpublished manuscript, Knoxville: University of Tennessee.

Gryeh, J. H., et al. (2000). Patterns of adjustment among children of battered women. *Journal of Consulting and Clinical Psychology, 68,* 84–94. Abstract retrieved August 15, 2003, from PsycINFO database.

Review

Sharpe, K. (2003, Summer). The whole world in your hands [Review of the book *World Atlas of Biodiversity*]. *Nature Conservancy, 53,* 86.

Hayes, E. B., & Piesman, J. (2003) How can we prevent Lyme disease? [rev. article]. *New England Journal of Medicine, 348,* 2,424–2,430.

Note: The Sharpe entry above shows the review of a book; the Hayes entry shows the review of several articles on a common theme.

Bibliography Form—Nonprint Material

Barstow, I. (2003, May 22). Palm reading as prediction [Interview]. Chattanooga, TN.

Ford, B., & Ford, S. (Producers). (2003). *Choreography on the
fly: Robert Royston & Lauree Baldovi* [Videotape].
Brentwood, CA: Images in Motion.

Excel 2003. (2003). [Computer software]. Redmond, WA:
Microsoft.

Abolitionist movement. (1999). *Compton's interactive
encyclopedia* [CD-ROM]. The Learning Company.

Bibliography Form—Internet Sources
Article from an Online Journal

Clune, A. C. (2002). Mental disorder and its cause.
Psycoloquy, 13. Retrieved September 23, 2003, from
http://psycprints.ecs.soton.ac.uk/archive/00000210/

Article from a Printed Journal, Reproduced Online

Many articles online are the exact duplicates of their printed versions, so if you view an article in its electronic form and are confident it is identical to the printed version, add within brackets the
words *Electronic version.* This allows you to omit the URL.

Bowler, D. M., & Thommen, E. (2000). Attribution of
mechanical and social causality to animated displays by
children with autism [Electronic version]. *Autism, 4,*
147–171.

Add the URL and date of access if page numbers are not
indicated.

Leshy, M. (2000). Missouri's savannas and woodlands. *Missouri
Conservationist, 61.* Retrieved August 30, 2003, from
http://www.conservation.state.mo.us/nonmag/2000/08/
1.htm

Article Retrieved from a Library Database

Colemen, L., & Coleman J. (2002). The measurement of
puberty: A review. *Journal of Adolescence, 25,* 535–550.
Retrieved April 2, 2004, from ERIC database
(EJ65060).

Abstract

Townsend, J. W. (2003). Reproductive behavior in the context
of global population. *American Psychologist, 58.*

Abstract retrieved October 13, 2003, from
http://www.apa.org/jounals/amp/303ab.html#2

Article from an Online Magazine, No Author Listed

Housing market fueled by rising consumer confidence, low
rates. (2003, June 12). *Builder Online.* Retrieved June
12, 2003, from http://www.builderonline.com/pages/
builderonline/Story.nsp?story_id=39428052&ID=
builderonline&scategory=Computers&type=news

Article from an Online Newspaper

Ippolito, M. (2003, June 12). Delta Moon rising locally.
Atlanta Journal-Constitution Online. Retrieved June
12, 2003, from http://www.accessatlanta.com/hp/
content/entertainment/features/0603/12delta.html

Bulletin

Murphy, F. L., M.D. (2003). What you don't know can hurt
you. *Preventive Health Center.* Retrieved October 19,
2003, from http://www.mdphc.com/ education/fiber.html

Document from a Government Agency

U.S. Cong. House. (2003, January 7). Unlawful Internet
gambling funding prohibition act. *House Resolution 21.*
Retrieved September 18, 2003, from http://thomas.loc.gov/
cgi-bin/query/D?c108:2:./temp/~c108k7golG::

Document from a University Program or Department

Spence, S. (2004). *Department of Humanities: Writing
criteria.* Retrieved January 25, 2004, from Clayton
College and State University, Department of Humanities
Web site http://a-s.clayton.edu/humanities/

Documents from Discussion Groups

Lettevall, E. (2003, January 7). Analysis of small population
size. Population Discussion Group [Msg 43]. Message
posted to http://canuck.dnr.cornell.edu/HyperNews/
get/marked/marked/289/1.html

Cheramy, R. (2003, April 18). Inexpensive and easy site
hosting. Message posted to impressive.net/archives/
fogo/20030418170059.GA23011bougon.org

Walker, Z. (2004, January 5). Jefferson History Panel.
Message posted to Hawkins mailing list, archived at
http://www.hawkins.org/mailarchives.html

11f   Formatting a Paper in the APA Style

Place your materials in this order:

1. Title page
2. Abstract
3. Introduction, body, conclusion
4. References
5. Appendix

Title Page

In addition to your title, name, and academic affiliation, the title page should establish the running head that will appear on every page preceding the page number. See page 158 for an example of the title page in APA style.

Abstract

You should provide an abstract with every paper written in APA style. An abstract is a quick but thorough summary of the contents of your paper. It is read first and may be the only part read, so it must be accurate, self-contained, concise, nonevaluative, and coherent. See page 159 for an example.

Text of the Paper

Double-space throughout your entire paper. In contrast to MLA style, you *should* use subtitles as side heads and centered heads in your paper. Follow your instructor's guidelines for formatting your paper (e.g., margins, indentions, and use of fonts).

References

Prepare your list of references according to the designs shown in section 11e, pages 152–57. The list should include all sources that are available to others. Do not list personal correspondence or e-mail.

Appendix

The appendix is the appropriate place for material that is not germane to your text but nevertheless has pertinence to the study. Here you can present graphs, charts, study plans, observation and test results, and other matter that will help your reader understand the nature of your work.

11g Sample Paper in APA Style

The following paper demonstrates the format and style of a paper written to the standards of APA style. Marginal notations, below, explain specific requirements.

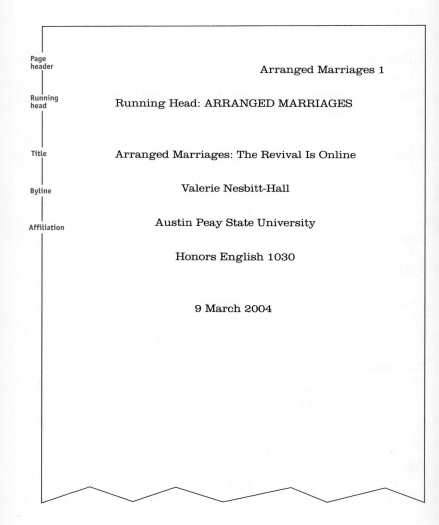

Page header

Running head

Title

Byline

Affiliation

Arranged Marriages 1

Running Head: ARRANGED MARRIAGES

Arranged Marriages: The Revival Is Online

Valerie Nesbitt-Hall

Austin Peay State University

Honors English 1030

9 March 2004

Arranged Marriages 2

Abstract

Computer matchmaking was investigated to examine the
theoretical implications of marriages arranged in part by
online dating. The goal was to determine the effect of Internet
activity on the private lives of participants. The social and
psychological implications were determined by an
examination of the literature, a profile of the participants, and
a case study that interviewed an affected couple. Results were
mixed with failures balanced against successful matches. The
social implications affect the workplace as well as the private
lives of the men and women who are active in chat rooms and
dating services. The psychological implications involve
infidelity, damage to self-esteem, the need for psychotherapy,
but—importantly—a chance for true and lasting love.

An abstract
is usually
required
for
scientific
writing.

Arranged Marriages 3

Arranged Marriages: The Revival Is Online

Arranged marriages are back, but with a twist. Online
dating services provide today, among other things, an
opportunity for people to meet, chat, reveal things about
themselves, and—as one source has expressed it—"play the
role of patriarchal grandfathers, searching for good matches
based on any number of criteria that you select" (Razdan,
2003, p. 71). Thus, computer matchmaking has social and
psychological implications that are being examined more and
more by psychologists. This paper will examine the theoretical
implications of marriages arranged in part by online dating.

Figures vary greatly on activity. One source (Cha, 2003)
reported that 37 million people used online matchmaking
services in April 2003, but another (Nussbaum, 2002) said

Establish the
topic along
with social
and or
psychological
issues that
will be
examined.

Arranged Marriages 4

only 15 million visited a dating site in all of 2002. Nevertheless, the figure is in the millions, and that is substantial. *People Weekly* (1999) reported that 50 million Americans were registered online, and that figure has climbed considerably since 1999. People have visited, many have found a mate, and some have even married. Match.com and America Online's dating area boast of hundreds of marriages that began as personal online messages. Can it be called a social revolution? Some have said "yes" to that question because about one-fifth of all singles in the country are online, prearranging their meetings and their lives, assuring themselves a better match than an evening's trip to a local nightclub. For example, Cooper (2002) argued that online dating has the potential to lower the nation's divorce rate. Kass (2003) identified the "distanced nearness" of a "protected (cyber)space that encourages self-revelation while maintaining personal boundaries" (cited in Razdan, 2003, p. 71).

The theoretical study depends heavily on the literature, which must be cited in correct APA form.

With the divorce rate at fifty percent, any marriage is already a roll of the dice, so experts have begun to agree that online dating reverts back to the prearranged meetings of two young people whom the families have identified as compatible for economic, political, religious, and social reasons. Persons online can enjoy distance, even hiding their real names for a while, to enjoy "an intimate but protected (cyber)space" (Kass, 2003, cited in Razdan, p. 71). Participants online can erect and maintain personal fences of privacy but at the same time reveal private feelings that they might never express in face-to-face meetings.

Method

Create major headings.

The Internet dating services have made romance a money-making enterprise. Match.com, founded in 1995 and now located in 27 countries, offers a subscription-based business model. Subscribers may place a personal advertisement for free, but to participate and send e-mail

Arranged Marriages 5

they must be members and pay about $20 per month. With several million active members, Match.com profits greatly from its primary commodity—romance. American Online, Yahoo!, Netscape—all the network servers offer the search machines, for a price, of course. "If you are prepared to pay a little—or a lot—it has never been easier to meet a partner," Brooks (2003) has said. But Brooks has also asked, "So why are so many people still single?" And then Brooks supplied this answer: "Perhaps the commodification of *romance* hasn't been as good for our hearts as it has for business."

Case Study

Research uncovered a match that resulted in marriage. The two subjects, Jennifer and Stephen, were interviewed on the matter of cyber romance. What follows is a brief summary of the interview, which is on file. The couple met online in September of 1996 in a chat room, not on a matching service. Stephen initiated the first contact, and they chatted anonymously for nine months before Jennifer initiated an exchange of phone numbers, addresses, and photographs. Stephen initiated the first meeting in person after 11 months, inviting Jennifer to travel from the United States to Glasgow, Scotland. Seven months later they married; it was 1.5 years from the time they met at the Internet newsgroup.

Scientific papers demand your explanations of procedures used in the study.

See page 48 for methods of conducting interviews.

When asked if online romance gave her protection of her privacy and time to prearrange things, Jennifer answered in the affirmative with emphasis. When asked who was more aggressive in pushing forward the romance, Stephen said it was a mutual thing. Both agreed that when they finally met in person, they really knew the other person—spiritually, emotionally, and intellectually. The matter of different nationalities also played a role on two fronts—immigration matters and the concern of Jennifer's parents that she would fly to Scotland to see someone she had never met.

Arranged Marriages 6

When asked if the relationship had been excellent to this point, both replied with affirmative answers. When asked if they would recommend online dating to others who are seeking mates, Stephen and Jennifer said, yes, under the right circumstances—"be cautious and take your time."

Results

In many instances, the results section includes tables, charts, and statistics.

Results of online romance can be positive or negative. First, the negative. Miller (1996) said:

> There's a big group of married baby boomers. When we look at ourselves in the mirror in our 40s, we wonder, "Am I still sexy?" Some women get facelifts; men get sports cars. Online infatuation can be another antidote. . . . From my research, only about one in four online relationships turns out happy. People get into this bodice-ripper mentality in the beginning. But after you've had "sex" with somebody in the virtual way, there's a real desire to actually be intimate. When the two do meet, the relationship can't handle the reality. Either the affair ends or it destroys their marriages. (p. 39)

Yet, as shown by the case study, online romances can have happy endings.

Discussion

The effects of online romance reach into the workplace as well as the personal lives of men and women in a variety of ways, both socially and psychologically.

Social Implications

Indented paragraph headings should be in italics and end with a period.

The woman's role. The woman must identify her role in relationship to the men in her life. In that regard, Bloom (1993) said:

> Even the most independent-minded erotic man becomes dependent on the judgment of a woman,

Arranged Marriages 7

> and a serious woman, one who is looking not only for an attractive man but for one who will love her and protect her, may be the best possible judge of a man's virtues and thus be regarded by even the most serious man as the supreme tribunal of his worth. (p. 104)

Cooper (2002) has observed that "the medium forces potential partners to talk, which," he says, "is something women in particular seem to want to do." Thus, although men frequent the Web sites more than women, the women may benefit at the higher rate, in part because they are more cautious and because anonymity gives them time to prearrange any meeting.

The man's role. Times they are a-changin'. Women as much as men are cruising the Internet, and women are more serious than the men. The typical male enters the Internet dating service thinking about sex, but he encounters women thinking about a relationship. The two are not entirely antithetical, but the timing varies, and the man discovers on the Internet that the woman controls much of the timing. "They do not realize," Kass (1999) has explained, "that what they need is courtship or something like it." Perhaps that's what men have begun to learn by online romance.

Psychological Implications

It is too soon, perhaps, to understand the full ramifications of online romance. Certainly, people have been severely wounded, both psychologically and physically, by venturing onto the Internet and getting trapped into damaging and fatal liaisons. At the same time, the ability to prearrange a meeting after weeks and months of conversation has its benefits. A man or woman who ventures onto the Internet will expose themselves to some of the same dangers as a blind date, except for the built-in firewalls between a username on the Web and somebody actually knocking on the door, ready for a date.

Arranged Marriages 8

Escape and damage to self-esteem. "Affairs can be a betrayal of the self and can imply that a person is avoiding knowing himself/herself or the partner when substituting fantasy sex online for a real relationship" (Maheu, 1999). A woman at midnight escapes into her addiction with an online lover, and man she has never met who may not even be a man, and she pretends the next day, as she serves breakfast to her family, that all is well. The damage to her psyche is like the early morning "walk of shame" that some young women experience—that return alone to their rooms from some encounter while the man curls up in bed with a smile on his face.

Psychotherapy. Participants in the online dating game can become depressed, angry, lose self-esteem, and go in search of psychotherapy. Cooper (2002), who is director of the San Jose Marital and Sexuality Centre, has reported that marital counseling is "exploding" because of fallouts from one partner's enticement into sex on the Internet, either the pornography or the online romance or the all-night chat sessions.

In conclusion, the world of online romance is growing at a staggering rate, with millions signing on each year and with thousands finding happiness and with thousands more finding chaos. Maheu (1999) has discussed methods of helping clients, even to the point of counseling in cyberspace itself, which would establish professional relationships online. Schneider and Weiss (2001) describe online addiction but offer little psychoanalysis. Cooper (2002) has an excellent collection of articles in his guidebook for clinicians. Counseling needs to be in place for persons who substitute fantasy sex online for a true relationship. However, numerous case studies also show that online romance can produce healthy relationships and successful marriages.

The conclusion often includes a statement on the state of research in the area of study.

Arranged Marriages 9

References

Bloom, A. (1993). *Love and friendship.* New York: Simon & Schuster.

Brooks, D. (2003). Dating on the Internet has come of age. *International Herald Tribune Online.* Retrieved April 9, 2003, from http://www.iht.com

Cha, A. E. (2003, May 4). ISO Romance? Online matchmakers put love to the test. *Washington Post,* p. A01. Retrieved April 9, 2003, from Lexis-Nexis database.

Cooper, A. (Ed.). (2002). *Sex and the Internet: A guidebook for clinicians.* New York: Brunner-Routledge.

Kass, A. A. (1999). A case for courtship. Address delivered to the Institute for American Values. New York: IAV.

Maheu, M. M. (1999). Women's Internet behavior: Providing psychotherapy offline and online for cyber-infidelity. Paper presented at the Annual Conference of the American Psychological Association, Boston, MA. Abstract retrieved April 9, 2003, from http://telehealth.net/articles/women/internet.html

Miller, M. (1996, April 8). Love at first byte. *People Weekly, 45,* 39. Retrieved April 5, 2003, from InfoTrac database.

Nussbaum, E. (2002, December 15). The year in ideas: Online personals are cool. *New York Times,* sec. 6, p. 106. Retrieved April 8, 2003, from http://www.nytimes.com

Razdan, A. (2003, May–June). What's love got to do with it? *Utne,* pp. 69–71.

Schneider, J., & Weiss, R. (2001). *Cybersex exposed: Simple fantasy or obsession?* Center City, MN: Hazelden.

References begin on a new page.

Citation for a conference presentation

Arranged Marriages 10

They've got love. (1999, February 15). *People Weekly, 51*, 45–52. Retrieved April 4, 2003, from InfoTrac database.

12

The Footnote System: CMS Style

The fine arts and some fields in the humanities, but not literature, use traditional footnotes, which should conform to standards set by *The Chicago Manual of Style* (CMS), 15th ed., 2003. In the CMS system, you must place superscript numerals within the text (like this[15]), and place documentary footnotes on corresponding pages.

The discussion below assumes that notes will appear as footnotes, but some instructors accept endnotes—that is, all notes placed together at the end of the paper rather than at the bottom of individual pages (see page 173).

12a Blending Sources into Your Writing

Two types of footnotes are available: the *documentary note* identifies your sources with bibliographic information and the other, called a *content note,* discusses related matters, explains your methods of research, suggests related literature, provides biographical information, or offers other information not immediately pertinent to your discussion. Both types are discussed in this chapter.

Introducing the Sources

The first example below implies a source that will be found in the footnote; the second expresses the name in the text. With footnotes, the implied reference is acceptable. With endnotes, however, you should probably use the expressed reference.

Implied reference:

The organic basis of autism is generally agreed upon. Three possible causes for autism have been identified: behavioral syndrome, organic brain disorder, or a range of biological and psychosocial factors.[9]

Expressed reference:

Martin Rutter has acknowledged that the organic basis of autism is generally agreed upon. Rutter named three possible causes for autism: behavioral syndrome, organic brain disorder, or a range of biological and psycho social factors.[10]

Inserting a Superscript Numeral in Your Text

Place Arabic numerals typed slightly above the line (like this[12]) with the superscript feature of your word processor. Place a superscript number immediately at the end of each quotation or paraphrase, without a space after the final word or mark of punctuation, as in this sample:

Steven A. LeBlanc, an archaeologist at Harvard University, along with several other scholars, argues that "humans have been at each others' throats since the dawn of the species."[1] Robin Yates, for example, says the ancient ancestors of the Chinese used "long-range projectile weapons" as long ago as 28,000 BC for both hunting and "intrahuman conflict."[2]

The footnotes that relate to these in-text superscript numerals will appear at the bottom of the page, as shown here:

1. Steven A. LeBlanc, "Prehistory of Warfare," *Archaeology* (May/June, 2003), 18.

2. Robin Yates, "Early China," in *War and Society in the Ancient and Medieval Worlds,* ed. Kurt Raaflaub and Nathan Rosenstein (Cambridge, MA: Center for Hellenic Studies, 1999): 9.

Writing Full or Abbreviated Notes

CMS style permits you to omit a bibliography page as long as you give full data to sources in each of your initial footnotes.

1. James W. Hall, *Rough Draft* (New York: St. Martin's Press, 2000), 49.

As an alternative, you may provide a comprehensive bibliography to each source at the end of the paper, in which case you can abbreviate the information in first footnotes.

1. Hall, 49.

The reader will find a complete citation in your bibliography entry at the end of the paper.

Hall, James W. *Rough Draft*. New York: St. Martin's Press, 2000.

12b Formatting and Writing the Footnotes

Place the text of a footnote on the same page as the corresponding superscript numeral. Single-space footnote text, but double-space between the notes. Indent the first line of each footnote or endnote five spaces. Number the notes consecutively throughout the entire paper. Use a raised superscript numeral for the in-text citation. Use a normal number for the text of the note. Separate footnotes from the text by triple-spacing or, if you prefer, by a twelve-space line from the left margin.

Article from a Journal

1. Gar Smith, "Water Wars, Water Cures," <u>Earth Island Journal</u> 15 (2003): 30.

Article from a Magazine

2. Leslie Allen, "Comparing Notes with Lewis and Clark," <u>American Heritage</u>, May 2003, 45.

Article from a Newspaper

3. Rhonda Abrams, "Latest FCC Deregulation Move Hurts Small Businesses," <u>Tennessean</u> (Nashville), May 18, 2003, 3E.

4. John Kifner, "The Holiest City, the Toughest Conflict," <u>New York Times</u>, July 23, 2000, sec. 4, p. 1.

Note: The abbreviations *sec.* and *p.* are necessary to distinguish the 4 and the 1.

Article or Selection from a Collection or Anthology

5. Sandra Leiblum and Nicola Döring, "Internet Sexuality: Known Risks and Fresh Chances for Women," in <u>Sex and the Internet: A Guidebook for Clinicians</u>, ed. Al Cooper (New York: Brunner-Routledge, 2002), 20–21.

Biblical Reference

6. Matt. 10.5

7. 1 Pet. 5:1–3 (NRSV).

Book

8. Steven A. LeBlanc, <u>Constant Battles: The Myth of the Peaceful, Noble Savage</u> (New York: St. Martin's Press, 2003), 20–23.

List two authors without a comma:

9. Doug Sulpy and Ray Schweighardt, <u>Get Back: The Unauthorized Chronicle of the Beatles "Let It Be" Disaster</u> (New York: St. Martin's Press, 1999), 18.

List three authors separated by commas. *Note:* Publisher's names are spelled out in full, but the words *Company* and *Inc.* are omitted.

10. James S. Mickelson, Karen S. Haynes, and Barbara Mikulski, <u>Affecting Change: Social Workers in the Political Arena</u>, 4th ed. (Boston: Allyn and Bacon, 2000), 340–41.

For more than three authors, use *and others* or *et al.* after mention of the lead author:

11. Nina Baym and others, eds., "Introduction," <u>Norton Anthology of American Literature</u>, 6th ed. (New York: Norton, 2003), 4.

Encyclopedia Entry

12. *The World Book Encyclopedia.* 2000 ed., s.v. "Raphael."

Film on DVD

13. *Titanic,* DVD, directed by James Cameron (1997; Hollywood, CA: Paramount Pictures, 1998).

Government Document

14. U.S. Dept. of the Treasury, "Financial Operations of Government Agencies and Funds," *Treasury Bulletin,* Washington, DC, June 1974, 134–41.

Lecture

15. Dick Weber, "The Facts About Preparing Teens to Drive" (lecture, Morrow High School, Morrow, GA, May 9, 2003).

Musical Work on VHS

16. Handel, George Frederic, *Messiah,* selections, VHS, Atlanta Symphony Orchestra and Chamber Chorus, Robert Shaw, conductor (Batavia, OH: Video Treasures, 1999).

Review Article

17. Audrey Webb, review of *Change Activist: Make Big Things Happen Fast,* by Carmel McConnell, *Earth Island Journal* (Summer 2003) 41.

Television Program

18. Dan Rather, *CBS News,* September 2, 2003.

12c   Writing Footnotes for Electronic Sources

To cite electronic sources, *The Chicago Manual of Style* requires the inclusion of a publication date, if it is available, and the URL, but not the date of access. The models below show these requirements.

Article Online

1. Arthur Ferrill, "Neolithic Warfare," Frontline Educational Foundation, http://eserver.org/history/neolithic-war.txt.

Article Reproduced Online

2. Ben Harder, "Ancient Peru Torture Deaths: Sacrifices or War Crimes?" *National Geographic News,* April 29, 2002, http://news.nationalgeographic.com/new/2002/04/0425_020426_mochekillings.html.

3. B. A. Miller, N. J. Smyth, and P. J. Mudar, "Mothers' Alcohol and Other Drug Problems and Their Punitiveness Toward Their Children," *Journal of Studies on Alcohol* 60 (1999): 632–42, http://www.ncbi.nlm.hih.gov.htbin.

Article Accessed from a Database through the Library System

4. Victor Davis Hanson, "War Will Be War: No Matter the Era, No Matter the Weapons, and the Same Old Hell," *National Review* 54 (2002), http://web4.infotrac.galegroup.com.

Book Online

5. D. H. Lawrence, *Lady Chatterley's Lover* (1928), http://bibliomania.com/fiction/dhl/chat.html.

CD-ROM Source

6. *Family Lawyer*. (Novato, CA: Broderbund, 2003). CD-ROM.

Electronic Bulletin Board, Archived Online

7. Warren Watts, e-mail to Victorian Association for Library Automation mailing list, September 23, 2003, http://www.vala.org.au/conf2004.htm.

E-mail

Since e-mail is not retrievable, do not document with a footnote. Instead, identify the source within your text.

Scholarly Project

8. *British Poetry Archive,* eds. Jerome McGann and David Seaman (University of Virginia Library, 1999), http://etext.lib.virgina.edu/britpo.html.

12d Writing Subsequent Footnote References

After a first full footnote, references to the same source should be shortened to author's last name and page number. When citing two works by an author, add a shortened version of the title: "3. Jones, *Paine,* 25." You may use *Ibid.* alone or with a page number, as shown below. If the subsequent note does not refer to the one immediately above it, do not use *Ibid.* Instead, repeat the author's last name (note especially the difference between notes 4 and 6):

3. Jerrold Ladd, *Out of the Madness: From the Projects to a Life of Hope* (New York: Warner, 1994), 24.

4. Ibid., 27.

5. Michael Schulman and Eva Meckler, *Bringing Up a Moral Child,* rev. ed. (New York: Doubleday, 1994), 221.

6. Ladd, 24.

12e   Writing Endnotes Rather Than Footnotes

With the permission of your instructor, put all your notes together as a single group of endnotes to lessen the burden of typing the paper. The list should be titled *Notes* and double-spaced throughout. Conform to the following example:

Notes

1. Jerrold Ladd, *Out of the Madness: From the Projects to a Life of Hope* (New York: Warner, 1994), 24.

2. Ibid., 27.

3. Michael Schulman and Eva Meckler, *Bringing Up a Moral Child,* rev. ed. (New York: Doubleday, 1994), 221.

4. W. V. Quine, *Word and Object* (Cambridge, MA: MIT Press, 1966), 8.

5. Schulman and Meckler, 217.

6. Abraham J. Heschel, *Man Is Not Alone: A Philosophy of Religion* (New York: Farrar, Straus, and Young, 1951), 221.

7. Ladd, 24.

12f   Writing Content Footnotes or Content Endnotes

As a general rule, put important matters in your text. Use content notes to explain research problems, conflicts in the testimony of the experts, matters of importance that are not germane to your discussion, interesting tidbits, credit to people and sources not mentioned in the text, and other matters that might interest readers. Two examples demonstrate the forms.

Related Matters Not Germane to the Text

1. The problems of politically correct language are explored in Adams, Tucker (4–5), Zalers, and also Young and

Smith (583). These authorities cite the need for caution by administrators who would impose new measures on speech and behavior.

Literature on a Related Topic

3. For additional study of the effects of alcoholics on children, see especially the *Journal of Studies on Alcohol* for the article by Wolin et al. and the bibliography on the topic by Orme and Rimmer (285–87). In addition, group therapy for children of alcoholics is examined in Hawley and Brown.

12g Writing a Bibliography Page for a Paper That Uses Footnotes

If you write completely documented footnotes, the bibliography is redundant. Type the first line of each entry flush left; indent the second line and other succeeding lines five spaces or 1 inch. Alphabetize the list by last names of authors. Double-space the entries as shown below. List alphabetically by title two or more works by one author. Here are the basic forms.

Book

Bryson, Bill. *A Short History of Nearly Everything*. New York: Broadway Books, 2003.

Journal Article

Damstra, Carolyn. "The Freer Gallery of Art." *Michigan History* 86 (2002): 46.

Newspaper

Abrams, Rhonda. "Latest FCC Deregulation Move Hurts Small Businesses." *Tennessean* (Nashville), May 18, 2003, 3E.

Internet Article

Ferrill, Arthur. "Neolithic Warfare," Frontline Educational Foundation. http://eserver.org/history/neolithic-war.txt.

12h   **Sample Research Paper in the CMS Style**

Johnston 1

Jamie Johnston

English Composition 1020

Professor Standiford

May 5, 2004

Prehistoric Wars: We've Always
Hated Each Other

Here we are, a civilized world with reasonably educated people, yet we constantly fight with each other. These are not sibling squabbles either; people die in terrible ways. We wonder, then, if there was ever a time when men and women lived in harmony with one another and with nature and the environment. The Bible speaks of the Garden of Eden, and the French philosopher Jean-Jacques Rousseau advanced the idea in the 1700s of the "noble savage," and that "nothing could be more gentle" than an ancient colony of people.[1] Wrong!

Steven A. LeBlanc, an archaeologist at Harvard University, along with several other scholars, argues instead that "humans have been at each others' throats since the dawn of the species."[2] Robin Yates, for example, says the ancient ancestors of the Chinese used "long-range projectile weapons" as long ago as 28,000 BC for both

---

1. See Steven A. LeBlanc, *Constant Battles: The Myth of the Peaceful, Noble Savage* (New York: St. Martin's Press, 2003), 15, and also L. D. Cooper, *Rousseau, Nature, and the Problem of the Good Life* (University Park: Pennsylvania State Univ. Press, 1999).

2. Steven A. LeBlanc, "Prehistory of Warfare," *Archaeology* (May/June, 2003), 18.

Marginal note: Name and course information precede the title. No separate title page is necessary unless you provide an outline, abstract, or other prefatory matter.

Johnston 2

hunting and "intrahuman conflict."[3] Arthur Ferrill observes, "When man first learned how to write, he already had war to write about."[4] Ferrill adds, "In prehistoric times man was a hunter and a killer of other men. The killer instinct in the prehistoric male is clearly attested by archaeology in fortifications, weapons, cave paintings, and skeletal remains."[5]

The writer uses the introduction to discuss historical evidence.

Evidence proves that savage fighting occurred in the ancient history of human beings. We have evidence of the types of weapons employed. We can also list reasons for the prehistoric fighting. This paper will examine those items, but the crux of the debate centers on the inducement or instinct. Were early humans motivated by biological instincts or by cultural demands for a share of limited resources? That's the issue this paper will address.

This section opens with the writer's thesis to introduce the issue.

First, we need to look briefly at the evidence. Ben Harder has reported on the work of one forensic anthropologist, John Verano, who has investigated a series of "grisly executions" in the valleys of Peru during the Moche civilization.[6] Victims "were apparently skinned alive.

---

3. Robin Yates, "Early China," in *War and Society in the Ancient and Medieval Worlds,* ed. Kurt Raaflaub and Nathan Rosenstein (Cambridge, MA: Center for Hellenic Studies, 1999): 9.

4. Arthur Ferrill, "Neolithic Warfare," Frontline Educational Foundation, http://eserver.org/history/neolithic-war.txt.

5. Ibid.

6. Cited in Ben Harder, "Ancient Peru Torture Deaths: Sacrifices or War Crimes?" *National Geographic News,* April 29, 2002, http://news.nationalgeographic.com/news/2002/04/0425_020426_mochekillings.html.

Johnston 3

Others were drained of blood, decapitated, or bound tightly and left to be eaten by vultures."[7] Verano has the proof of the executions, but not the reason, although speculations center on religious ceremonies. UCLA anthropologist Christopher B. Donnan has studied Moche art and suggests, "The suffering of the losers may have had a ritualistic meaning in Moche society much as the pain of Christ does in Christianity."[8] At the same time, Verano thinks the victims were prisoners of war and not the losers of ritual combat. In either case, the ancients were less than noble savages.

The weapons, too, have been uncovered: clubs, arrowheads, bows, slings, daggers, maces, and spears. Each weapon graduated upon the previous and served new purposes as armies gathered for combat. One source points out that "the bow and the sling were important for hunting, but the dagger and mace were most useful for fighting other humans."[9] The spear required close combat. The bow and arrow had a range of about 100 yards. The sling was a significant weapon because in the right hands it was accurate from long distances and very powerful with stones that could crush skulls. The mace gave way to the battle axe to cut through armor. Then with copper, bronze, and finally iron, the sword gained great popularity and remains a weapon of choice even today.[10]

Ultimately, the key question about the cause of war, whether ancient or current, centers on one's choice between

---

7. Ibid.

8. Christopher Donnan, cited in Harder.

9. "Prehistoric Warfare," http://digilander.libero.it/ tepec/prehistoric_warfare.htm.

10. Ibid.

Johnston 4

biology and culture. On the one side we have the historian, like Victor Hanson, who argues, "Culture largely determines how people fight. The degree to which a society embraces freedom, secular rationalism, consensual government, and capitalism often determines—far more than its geography, climate, or population—whether its armies will be successful over the long term."[11] Hanson adds, "No nation has ever survived once its citizenry ceased to believe that its culture was worth saving."[12]

The society as a whole wants to preserve its culture, in peace if possible. In 500 BC Herodotus said, "No one is so foolish that he prefers war to peace. In peace sons bury their fathers, in war fathers their sons."[13]

Yet, the biological history of men and women suggests that we love a good fight. I recall reading an article that said twins inside the womb actually fight, and one fetus might actually devour or absorb the other one. Siblings just naturally fight, as I did with my older sister and younger brother. His anger exploded one time, and he broke my arm by hitting me with a shovel. We all have witnessed the terrible fights at sporting events, and recently at Glenbrook North High School in Northbrook, Illinois, hazing turned into a terrible beating for some girls. Oh sure, we can give reasons for our eagerness to fight—to preserve our honor ("Don't diss me!"), to preserve our freedom ("Don't encroach!"), or because

---

11. Victor Davis Hanson, "War Will Be War: No Matter the Era, No Matter the Weapons, and the Same Old Hell," *National Review* 54 (2002), http://web4.infotrac.galegroup.com.

12. Ibid.

13. Qtd. in Peter Jones, "Ancient and Modern," *Spectator* 291 (2003), http://web.infotrac.galegroup.com.

Johnston 5

of fear ("Don't hit me 'cause I'll be hitting back even harder!"). Yet in a final analysis, people want power over others—men beat their wives, mothers overly spank their children, the better team overpowers an opponent, and, yes, a larger, stronger nation will demolish another if self-interest prevails.

This is human nature. The men of al-Quida who flew their suicide missions into the World Trade Center and the Pentagon knew exactly what they were doing—exercising their power. In effect, they said, "We'll show the United States that we can inflict great damage." Professor Donald Kagan observes:

> In the end what people really go to war about is
> power, by which I simply mean the ability to have
> their will prevail. . . . Every being and every nation
> requires power for two purposes. The first is to be
> able to do what it wishes to and must do, some of
> which will be good and perfectly natural things.
> Second, one needs power to keep others from
> imposing their will, to prevent evil things from
> being done.[14]

The sport of boxing continues to thrive, despite attempts to end it because of its brutality. The fans have a vicarious thrill as one boxer gets pounded to the canvas. At NASCAR races the greatest shouts occur as the fenders crash and cars go tumbling topsy-turvy down the asphalt. The aggressive behavior of humans is not always a pretty sight, such as the eager willingness of some to loot and pilfer a neighborhood that has been hit by a tornado or other natural disaster.

The writer's conclusion connects his thesis to the modern emphasis on war and terrorism.

---

14. Donald Kagan, "History's Largest Lessons" (interview by Fredric Smoler), *American Heritage* 48 (1997), http://web4.infotrac.galegroup.com.database.

Johnston 6

At the same time, a country like ours governs itself, imposing order by law and moral behavior by religion.[15] Our government, our culture, and our sense of honor have prevailed in a world of nations gone berserk and lawless. Whether we should use our power to impose our sense of democracy on other countries is an international question without a clear answer. My brother, with the shovel in his hand, would say "yes."

A separate bibliography page is not required if you provide full data in each of your initial footnotes.

---

15. When chaos develops, as in Baghdad during the Iraqi War, lawless looting and violence emerge because neither the religious leaders nor an absent police force can maintain order. The breakdown of the culture opens a vacuum filled quickly by primitive behavior.

13

CSE Style for the Natural and Applied Sciences

The Council of Scientific Editors has established a *number* system for writing in the applied sciences, such as chemistry, computer science, mathematics, physics, and the medical sciences. This system uses numbers in the text rather than a name and year.

> The original description (3) contained precise taxonomic detail that differed with recent studies (4–6).

The number system saves space, and the numbers minimally disrupt the reading of the text. But the number system seldom mentions names, so you must provide a bibliography.

13a Writing In-Text Citations Using the CSE Number System

Each source is assigned an identifying number. Use this style with these disciplines: chemistry, computer science, mathematics, physics, and the medical sciences (medicine, nursing, and general health).

After completing a list of references, assign a number to each entry. Use one of two methods for numbering the list: (1) arrange references in alphabetical order and number them consecutively (in which case the numbers will appear in random order in the text), or (2) number the references consecutively as you put them into your text, interrupting that order when entering references cited earlier.

The number will identify the source in the Cited References. Conform to the following regulations:

1. Place the number within parentheses (1) or brackets [2] or as a raised index numeral, like this.[5] A name is not required and is even discouraged, so try to arrange your wording accordingly.

Place full information on the author and the work in the references list.

It is known (1) that the DNA concentration of a nucleus doubles during interphase.

A recent study [1] has raised interesting questions related to photosynthesis, some of which have been answered [2].

In particular, a recent study[1] has raised many interesting questions related to photosynthesis, some of which have been answered.[2]

2. If the sentence uses the authority's name, add the number after the name.

Additional testing by Cooper (3) includes alterations in carbohydrate metabolism and changes in ascorbic acid incorporation into the cell and adjoining membranes.

3. If necessary, add specific data to the entry:

The results of the respiration experiment published by Jones (3, Table 6, p 412) had been predicted earlier by Smith (5, Proposition 8).

13b Writing the References Page

Supply a list of references at the end of your paper. Number it to correspond to sources as you cite them in the text. An alternate method is to alphabetize the list and then number it. Label the list *Cited References.* The form of the entries should duplicate the examples shown below.

Book

Provide a number and then list the author, title of the book, place of publication, publisher, year, and total number of pages (optional).

1. LeBlanc AN. Random family: Love, drugs, trouble, and coming of age. New York: Simon and Schuster; 2003. 416 p.

Article in a Journal

Provide a number and then list the author, the title of the article, the name of the journal, the year and month if necessary, volume number and issue number if necessary, and inclusive pages. The month or an issue number is necessary for any journal that is paged anew with each issue.

> 2. Renner R. Drams of drugs and dregs. Sci Am 2002 May; 286(5):29.

Internet Articles and Other Electronic Publications

Add at the end of the citation an availability statement as well as the date you accessed the material.

> 3. Shane-McWhorter L. Complementary and alternative medicine (CAM) in diabetes. Complementary and Alternative Med [online] 2002. Available from http://www.childrenwithdiabetes.com/ clinic/alternative. Accessed 2003 Aug 8.

Magazine or Newspaper Article

Add a specific date and, for newspapers, cite a section letter or number.

> 4. Murphy C, Haggerty R. Reinventing a river. Am Heritage 2003 Apr/May: 60–67.
> 5. [Anonymous]. FDA approval of drug gives diabetics a new choice. Los Angeles Times 2000 Aug 2; Sect A:4.

Proceedings and Conference Presentations

After supplying a number, give the name of the author or editor, title of the presentation, name of the conference, type of work (report, proceedings, proceedings online, etc.), name of the organization or society, date of the conference, and place. If found on the Internet, add the URL and the date you accessed the information.

> 6. Ashraf H, Banz W, Sundberg J. Soyful luncheon: Setting a healthful table for the community [abstract online]. In: Crossing Borders: Food and Agriculture in the Americas. Proceedings online of the Assn for the Study of Food and Soc; 1999 June 3–6; Toronto (ON). Available from http://www.acs.ryerson.ca/ foodsec/foodsec/papers.html. Accessed 2003 Aug 8.

Article from a Loose-Leaf Collection

> 7. [Anonymous]. No-till farming shows skeptics the advantages of giving up the plow. CQ Researcher 1994;4:1066.

13c Sample Paper Using the CSE Numbering System

Diabetes Management:
A Delicate Balance

Balance the title, name, and academic affiliation on a title page.

By
Sarah E. Bemis
English 103: College Writing
Sister Winifred Morgan, O.P.
5 December 2003

ii

Abstract

Diabetes affects approximately 11 million people in the U. S. alone, leading to \$350 billion in medical costs. Two types, I and II, have debilitating effects. The body may tolerate hyperglycemia for a short time, but severe complications can occur, such as arteriosclerosis, heart disease, nerve damage, and cerebral diseases. New drugs continue to improve the lifestyle of a person with diabetes, but controlling blood sugar requires three elements working together—medication, diet, and exercise. This study examines the importance of each of the three. Patients need a controlled balance of the medication, diet, and exercise program.

An abstract of 100–200 words states the purpose, scope, and major findings of the study.

1

Diabetes Management:

A Delicate Balance

Diabetes is a disease that affects approximately 11 million people in the U.S. alone. Diabetes and its complications lead to approximately 350,000 deaths per year and cost the nation $20,373 billion per year in medical care, in the direct cost of complications, and in the indirect costs of loss of productivity related to the disease (1). The condition can produce devastating side effects and a multitude of chronic health problems. For this reason, it can be very frightening to those who do not understand the nature and treatment of the disease. Diabetes currently has no known cure, but it can be controlled. By instituting a healthy, balanced lifestyle, most persons with diabetes can live free of negative side effects.

Diabetes mellitus, according to several descriptions, is a disorder in which the body cannot properly metabolize glucose or sugar. The body's inability to produce or properly use insulin permits glucose to build up in the bloodstream. The excess sugar in the blood, or hyperglycemia, is what leads to the side effects of diabetes (2, 3, 4).

There are actually two types of diabetes. Type I, or juvenile diabetes, is the name given to the condition in which the pancreas produces very little or no insulin. Type II diabetes occurs when the pancreas produces usable insulin, but not enough to counteract the amount of glucose in the blood.

In both Type I and Type II diabetes, the problem has been identified as hyperglycemia (5). This buildup of glucose in the bloodstream leads to a number of dangerous side effects. The amount of glucose the kidneys can filter varies with each person. In this process, all the water in the body's tissues is being used to produce urine to flush glucose from the kidneys. This is what leads to the intense thirst and frequent urination associated with hyperglycemia (5). The glucose

---

Use a number to register the use of a source.

The thesis or hypothesis is expressed usually at the end of the introduction.

Scientific writing requires precise definition.

More than one source can be listed for one idea or concept.

Causal analysis, as shown here, is a staple of scientific writing.

2

cannot be processed to produce energy. The cells signal the brain that they are not getting sugar and this causes hunger. However, no matter how much a victim of hyperglycemic diabetes eats, the cells will not be producing energy (6).

Refer to sources in the past tense or present perfect tense.

It has been shown (4) that the kidneys attempt to filter the sugar from the blood, so the liver tries to produce energy by burning fat and muscle to produce ketones, a protein that the body burns in place of glucose. Ketones do not provide the energy the body requires but do produce chemicals toxic to the body. Too many ketones can poison the blood (4) and result in frequent urination, dry mouth, extreme thirst, headache, rapid and deep respiration, increased heart rate, nausea, vomiting, disorientation, and lethargy (1).

It has also been reported (7) that the immune system is also affected and that victims experience infection more often and more severely than a person without diabetes. Other conditions that frequently occur in conjunction with hyperglycemia in its early stages are depression and chronic fatigue (8). Many patients who experience hyperglycemia have difficulties controlling gain and loss of weight as well.

Arteriosclerosis occurs in hyperglycemic diabetics over time, resulting in decreased circulation and eyesight. This also may lead to heart disease, angina, and heart attack, the most prevalent causes of death among diabetics (1). Also common is diabetic neuropathy, a degeneration of the nerves. This condition causes pain and loss of function in the extremities (1).

A person with diabetes is also at risk for many cerebral diseases and kidney infections (1). However, all of these effects can be reduced, delayed, and even prevented with proper care and control. By monitoring blood sugar and reacting accordingly with medication, by special diets, and by exercise and a controlled lifestyle, persons with diabetes can avoid these serious health conditions (Brancati and others 9).

3

The first aspect of diabetes care is blood sugar monitoring and medication. The two go hand in hand in that the patient must have the appropriate type and dosage of medication and must know blood sugar values and patterns in order to determine the correct regimen. Two main types of monitoring are necessary for diabetes control. Patients must perform home glucose monitoring on a daily basis with electronic equipment.

In addition to daily monitoring, doctors usually perform a test called a hemoglobin AIC, which gives a better indication of blood sugar control over a longer period of time than a home test. This should be done approximately every ninety days, as that is the time period over which blood cells are renewed.

The treatment of diabetes usually involves medication. Since Type I diabetics produce very little or no insulin, insulin injections will always be necessary. For Type II, the treatment may be strictly dietary, dietary with oral hypoglycemic agents, or insulin therapy.

The writer explores the first method for controlling diabetes—medication.

Some Type II patients can control the disease with a combination of diet, exercise, and an oral hypoglycemic agent. These drugs themselves contain no insulin. They traditionally lower blood glucose levels by stimulating the pancreas to produce insulin (10). Therefore, they are only appropriate for patients whose pancreas is still producing some insulin. Some new drugs may be becoming available in the new millennium. Creators of the pharmaceuticals are able to increase sensitivity to insulin and suppress the secretion of hormones that raise blood sugar.

While it is important to have the proper medication, the backbone of diabetes management is the meal plan. By making wise choices in eating, persons with diabetes can reduce stress on the body and increase the effectiveness of their medication. The basis of a good meal plan is balanced nutrition and moderation. Eating a low-fat, low-sodium,

The writer explores the second method for controlling diabetes—diet.

4

low-sugar diet is the best way for a diabetic to ensure longevity and health.

Three meal plans are recommended for patients (11). The Food Pyramid divides food into six groups. These resemble the traditional four food groups, except that they are arranged in a pyramid in which the bottom, or largest, section contains the foods that should be eaten most each day. The top, or smallest, section contains the foods that should be eaten least, if at all.

The Exchange Plan provides a very structured meal plan. Foods are divided into eight categories, which are more specific than those of the Food Pyramid. A dietician or physician determines a daily calorie range for the patient and, based on that range, decides how many servings she or he should eat from each category per meal.

Another meal plan is carbohydrate counting. Once again, food is categorized, but into only three groups. The largest food group, carbohydrates, encompasses not only starches, but dairy products, fruits, and vegetables as well. The dietician or physician again assigns a calorie range. With this plan, however, only the number of carbohydrates per meal are assigned, and even this is flexible (5, 10).

The writer explores the third method for controlling diabetes—exercise.

The final element in successfully managing diabetes is exercise. It has been shown (11) that exercise can help stimulate the body to use glucose for energy, thus taking it out of the blood. Something as simple as a walking routine can significantly reduce blood glucose levels (11). Some patients may require as little as a 15-minute per day walk, where some may need a more involved workout.

All of the aspects of diabetes management can be summed up in one word: balance. Diabetes itself is caused by a lack of balance of insulin and glucose in the body. In order to restore that balance, a person with diabetes must juggle medication, monitoring, diet, and exercise. Managing diabetes is not an easy task, but a long and healthy life is very possible when the delicate balance is carefully maintained.

5

Cited References

1. Guthrie DW, Guthrie RA. Nursing management of diabetes mellitus. New York: Springer; 1991. 241 p.

2. [Anonymous]. Diabetes insipidus. Am Acad of Family Phys. Available from http://www.aafp.org/patientinfo/insipidu.html. Accessed 2000 Aug 10.

3. Clark CM, Fradkin JE, Hiss RG, Lorenz RA, Vinicor F, Warren-Boulton E. Promoting early diagnosis and treatment of type 2 diabetes. JAMA 2000;284:363–365.

4. [Anonymous]. Do you know your blood-sugar level? Consumer Reports on Health 2000;12(7):1–4.

5. Gehling E. The family and friends' guide to diabetes: Everything you need to know. New York: Wiley; 2000. 282 p.

6. Schlosberg S. The symptoms you should never ignore. Shape 2000 Aug; 19:136–142.

7. Espenshade JE. Staff Manual for Teaching Patients About Diabetes Mellitus. Chicago: Amer Hospital Assn., 1979. 192 p.

8. Roberts SS. The diabetes advisor. Diabetes Forecast 2000;53:41–42. Available from http://www.diabetes.org/diabetesforecast/00August/default.asp. Accessed 2000 Aug 8.

9. Brancati FL, Kao WHL, Folsom AR, Watson RL, Szklo M. Incident type 2 diabetes mellitus in African American and white adults. JAMA 2000;283:2253–2259.

10. Nurses' Clinical Library. Endocrine Disorders. Springhouse, PA: Springhouse; 1984. 183 p.

11. [Anonymous]. Exercise. Am Diabetes Assn 2000. Available from http://www.diabetes.org/exercise. Accessed 2000 Aug 11.

Cited references appear by the number sequence of presentation in the book.

14

Preparing Electronic Research Projects

Creating your research paper electronically has a number of advantages:

- **It uses the newest technology.**
- **It offers multimedia potential.**
- **It can link your reader to more information.**

14a Using Word Processing to Create Electronic Documents

The easiest way to create an electronic document is by using word processing programs such as Microsoft Word® or Corel WordPerfect® and then distributing your report in its electronic form rather than printing it out. (See Figure 14.1 for an example of how such a research paper might look.)

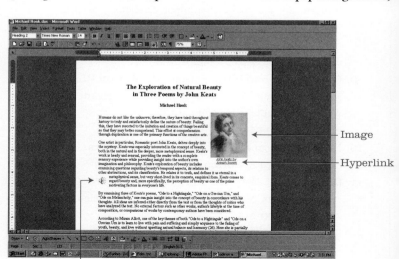

Image

Hyperlink

Sound link

■ FIGURE 14.1

Word processed research paper.

190

14b Building a Slide Show

If you plan an oral presentation, an electronic slide show can help illustrate your ideas. Electronic presentations differ from word processed documents in that each page, or slide, constitutes one computer screen. The reader clicks to move to the next slide (see Figure 14.2).

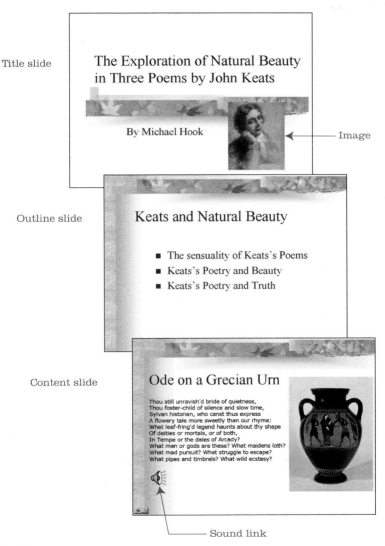

FIGURE 14.2
Research paper slide presentation.

Since each slide can hold only limited information, condense your content.

14c Creating Pages with Hypertext Markup Language (HTML)

Creating a Web page or a Web site involves collecting or making a series of computer files—some of them the HTML files that contain the basic text and layout for your pages, and others that contain the graphics, sounds, or video that go with them.

Using a Web Page Editor to Create Web Pages

The easiest way to create pages is with a Web page editor such as Microsoft FrontPage®, Adobe Page Mill®, or Netscape Composer®. These programs work differently, but they all do the same thing—create Web pages. Using them is like using a word processor: you enter or paste in text, insert graphics or other multimedia objects, and save the file to disk. You can also specify fonts, font sizes, font styles (like bold), alignment, lists with bullets, and numbered lists. Here are a few tips for entering text into a Web page:

- Use bold rather than underlining for emphasis and titles. On a Web site, links are underlined, so any other underlining may cause confusion.
- Do not use tabs. HTML does not support tabs for indenting the first line of a paragraph. You also won't be able to use hanging indents for your bibliography.
- Do not double-space. The Web page editor automatically single-spaces lines of text and double-spaces between paragraphs.
- Make all lines flush left on the Works Cited page; HTML does not support hanging indentions.

When the word processing software converts your document to HTML, it also converts any graphics you've included to separate graphics files. Together, your text and the graphics can be viewed in a Web browser like any other Web page (see Figure 14.3).

Your research paper will look somewhat different in HTML format than in its word processed format. In some ways, HTML is less flexible than word processing, but you can still use word processing software to make changes to your HTML-formatted paper.

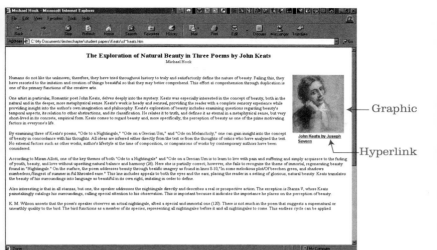

— Graphic

—Hyperlink

FIGURE 14.3
Single Web page research paper.

HINT: For more information on building Web pages and sites, see the following Web site: NCSA Beginner's Guide to HTML **http://www.ncsa.uiuc.edu/general/internet/www/ htmlprimer.html**.

Citing Your Sources in a Web Research Paper

If you are using MLA, APA, or CSE styles, include parenthetical citations in the text itself and create a separate Web page for references. Remember to include such a page in your plans and to provide hyperlinks pointing to it from various places in the paper. If you are using the CMS footnote system, do not put footnotes at the bottom of each of your Web pages. Instead, create a separate page that holds all the notes, just as you would in MLA or APA with Works Cited or References pages respectively. Create each footnote number as a link to this Notes page so readers can click on the number to go to the note. Remember to have a link on the Notes page to return the reader to the text.

Using Graphics in Your Electronic Research Paper

GIF stands for Graphical Interchange Format, which develops and transfers digital images. JPEG stands for Joint Photographic Experts Group, which compresses color images to smaller files for ease of transport.

In general, JPEGs work best for photographs and GIFs work best for line drawings. To save a file as a GIF or JPEG, open it in an image-editing program like Adobe Photoshop® and save the file as one of the two types (for example, keats.jpg or keats.gif).

Programs usually also have menu commands for inserting graphics; refer to your user documentation to find out how to do so.

Creating Your Own Digital Graphics

Making your own graphics file is complex but rewarding, and it adds a personal level of creativity to your research paper. Use one of the following techniques:

- **Use a graphics program,** such as Macromedia Freehand® or Adobe Illustrator®. With such software you can create a graphics file and save it in JPEG or GIF format.
- **Use a scanner** to copy your drawings, graphs, photographs, and other matter. Programs such as Adobe Photoshop® and JASC Paintshop Pro® are useful for modifying scanned photographs.
- **Create original photographs with a digital camera.** Digital cameras usually save images as JPEGs, so you won't need to convert the files into a usable format.

As long as you create JPEG files or GIF files for your graphics, you can transport the entire research paper to a Web site.

Delivering Your Electronic Research Paper to Readers

Follow your instructor's requirements for delivering your electronic research paper, or use one of the techniques in the following checklist.

CHECKLIST

Delivering Your Electronic Research Paper

- **Floppy disk.** Floppy disks are a convenient way to share information. However, they are unreliable, and papers with graphics, sound, or video may not fit on a disk.

- **Zip disk.** A Zip disk or other proprietary format holds much larger files than a floppy disk does, but your reader/professor must own a drive that can read it.

- **CD-ROM disks.** These disks hold large amounts of data and thus work well for transmitting graphics, sound, or video files. However, you must own or have access to a CD-R (Compact Disk Recordable) or CD-RW (Compact Disk Recordable/Writable) drive. Most readers have regular CD-ROM drives that can read your disks, but you might want to confirm this beforehand.

- **E-mail.** E-mailing your file as an attachment is the fastest way to deliver your electronic research paper; however, this approach works best if you have a single file, like a word processed research paper, rather than a collection of related files, like a Web site.

- **Web site.** If you've created a Web site or Web page, you can upload your work to a Web server, and readers can access your work on the Internet. Procedures for uploading Web sites vary from school to school and server to server; work closely with your instructor and Webmaster to perform this process successfully. Regardless of the method you choose, be sure to follow your instructor's directions and requirements.

APPENDIX
Glossary of
Manuscript Style

The alphabetical glossary that follows answers most of your miscellaneous questions about matters of form, such as margins, pagination, dates, and numbers. For matters not addressed below, consult the index, which directs you to appropriate pages elsewhere in this text.

Abbreviations

Employ abbreviations often and consistently in notes and citations, but avoid them in the text. In your citations, but not in your text, always abbreviate these items:

- Technical terms and reference words (anon., e.g., diss.)
- Institutions (acad., assn., Cong.)
- Dates (Jan., Feb.)
- States and countries (OH, CA, U.S.A.)
- Names of publishers (McGraw, UP of Florida)
- Titles of literary works (*Ado* for *Much Ado about Nothing*)
- Books of the Bible (Exod. For Exodus)

Accent Marks

When you quote, reproduce accents exactly as they appear in the original.

"La tradición clásica en españa," according to Romana,
remains strong in public school instruction (16).

Ampersand

Avoid using the ampersand symbol "&" unless custom demands it (e.g., "A & P"). In MLA, CSE, and CMS style, use *and* for in-text citations (e.g., Smith and Jones 213–14). In APA style use "&" within parenthetical citations (e.g., Spenser & Wilson, 1994, p. 73) but not in the text (e.g., Spenser and Wilson found the results in error).

Arabic Numerals

Both the MLA style and the APA style require Arabic numerals whenever possible: for volumes, books, parts, and chapters of works; acts, scenes, and lines of plays; cantos, stanzas, and lines of poetry.

Numbers Expressed as Figures in Your Text

Use figures in your text according to the following examples:

- All numbers 10 and above
- Numbers that represent ages, dates, time, size, score, amounts of money, and numerals used as numerals
- Statistical and mathematical numbers
- Numbers that precede units of measurement
- Numbers below 10 grouped with higher numbers

Number Use with Symbols

Use numerals with appropriate symbols (3%, $5.60); otherwise, use numerals only when the number cannot be spelled out in one or two words:

one hundred percent *but* 150 percent
a two-point average *but* a 2.5 average
one metric ton *but* 0.907 metric ton or 3.150 metric tons
forty-five percent *but* 45 1/2 percent *or* 45 1/2%

In business, scientific, and technical writing that involves frequent use of percentages, write all of them as numerals with the appropriate symbol (100%, 12%).

Numbers Expressed in Words in Your Text

Spell out numbers in the following instances:

- Numbers less than 10 that are not used as measurements
- Common fractions
- Any number that begins a sentence
- References to centuries

Numbers as Both Words and Figures

Combine words and figures in these situations:

- Back-to-back modifiers:

    twelve 6-year-olds *or* 12 six-year-olds, *but not* 12 6-year olds

- Large numbers (4 million)

Bullets, Numbers, and Indented Lists

Computers supply several bullet and number list styles whose indented lines begin with a circle, square, diamond, triangle, number, or letter. Use this feature to make a list stand out in your text.

Capitalization

Capitalize Some Titles

For books, journals, magazines, and newspapers capitalize the first word, the last word, and all principal words, including words that follow hyphens in compound terms (e.g., French-Speaking Islands). Do not capitalize articles, prepositions that introduce phrases, conjunctions, and the *to* in infinitives when these words occur in the middle of the title (for example, *The Last of the Mohicans*). Some scholarly styles capitalize only the first word of and proper names in reference titles and subtitles. Study the appropriate style for your field.

Capitalize the first word after the colon when introducing a rule, maxim, or principle and when introducing a quotation that is independent of your main sentence.

When introducing a list or an elaboration on the idea of the first clause, do not capitalize the first word after the colon.

Use capitals for trade names such as Pepsi, Plexiglas, Dupont, Dockers, Thunderbird, and Nikon.

Capitalize proper names used as adjectives *but not* the words used with them: Einstein's theory, Salk's vaccine.

Capitalize the names of departments or courses, but use lowercase when they are used in a general sense.

Department of Psychology but the psychology department

Capitalize a noun that denotes a specific place in a numbered series but not nouns that name common parts of books.

Comma

Use commas between items listed in a series of three or more, including before the *and* and *or* that precedes the last item. For example:

Reader (34), Scott (61), and Wellman (615–17) agree with Steinbeck on this point.

Never use a comma and a dash together. The comma follows a parenthesis if your text requires the comma:

How should we order our lives, asks Thompson (22–23), when we face "hostility from every quarter"?

The comma goes inside single quotation marks as well as double quotation marks:

> Such irony is discovered in Smith's article, "The Sources of Franklin's 'The Ephemera,'" but not in most textual discussions.

Figures and Tables

A table is a systematic presentation of materials, usually in columns. A figure is any nontext item that is not a table: blueprint, chart, diagram, drawing, graph, photo, photostat, map, and so on. Use graphs appropriately. A line graph serves a different purpose than a circle (pie) chart, and a bar graph plots different information than a scatter graph. Place captions above a table and below a figure. Here is an example:

Table 1

Response by Class on Nuclear Energy Policy

	Freshmen	Sophomores	Juniors	Seniors
1. More nuclear power	150	301	75	120
2. Less nuclear power	195	137	111	203
3. Present policy is acceptable	87	104	229	37

Sample table

Foreign Cities

In general, spell the names of foreign cities as they are written in original sources. However, for purposes of clarity, you may substitute an English name or provide both with one in parentheses:

> Köln (Cologne)   Braunschweig (Brunswick)

Headings

Most papers require only major headings (A-level), but subheads are permitted (see the use of subheads on pages 158–64). Also examine the chart at the top of the next page.

Indenting

Indent paragraphs five spaces or 1/2 inch. Indent block quotations (four lines or more) ten spaces or 1 inch from the left margin. If your block

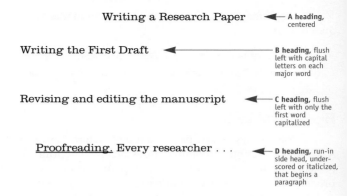

Writing a Research Paper ◄— **A heading,** centered

Writing the First Draft ◄ **B heading,** flush left with capital letters on each major word

Revising and editing the manuscript ◄— **C heading,** flush left with only the first word capitalized

<u>Proofreading.</u> Every researcher . . . ◄— **D heading,** run-in side head, under-scored or italicized, that begins a paragraph

quotation is one paragraph, do not indent the first line more than the rest. However, if your block quotation is two or more paragraphs, indent the first line of each paragraph an extra three spaces or 1/4 inch. Use a five-space hanging indention for entries of the Works Cited page. Indent the first line of footnotes five spaces. Other styles (APA and CSE) have different requirements (see Chapter 11, pages 148–66, and Chapter 13, pages 181–89).

Margins

A basic 1-inch margin on all sides of each page is recommended. Place your page number 1/2 inch below the top edge of the paper and 1 inch from the right edge. Your software has a ruler, menu, or style palette that allows you to set the margins. *Tip:* If you develop a header, the running head may appear 1 inch from the top, in which case your first line of text will begin 1 1/2 inches from the top.

Monetary Units

Spell out monetary amounts only if you can do so in three words or fewer. Conform to the following:

$12 *or* twelve dollars
$14.25 *but not* fourteen dollars and twenty-five cents
$8 billion *or* eight billion dollars
$10.3 billion *or* $10,300,000,000
$63 *or* sixty-three dollars

Names of Persons

At the first mention of a person, give the full name (e.g., Ernest Hemingway or Margaret Mead) and thereafter give only the surname, such as Hemingway or Mead. (APA style uses the last name only in the text.) Omit formal titles (Mr., Mrs., Dr., Hon.). Use simplified names of famous persons (e.g., Dante and Michelangelo rather than Dante Alighieri and

Michelangelo di Lodovico Buonarroti Simoni) when they are familiar. Use pseudonyms (e.g., George Eliot, Mark Twain, Stendhal). Use fictional names (e.g., Huck, Lord Jim, Santiago, Captain Ahab).

Numbering Pages

Number your pages in a running head in the upper right-hand corner of each. Depending on the software, you can create the head with the Numbering or the Header feature. See the sample papers for page numbers for MLA style, pages 141–47; APA style, pages 158–66; CMS style, pages 175–80; and CSE style, pages 184–89.

Roman Numerals

Use capital roman numerals for titles of persons (Elizabeth II) and major sections of an outline (see pages 81–83). Use lowercase roman numerals for preliminary pages of text, as for a preface or introduction (iii, iv, v). Otherwise, use Arabic numerals (e.g., Vol. 5, Act 2, Ch. 17, Plate 21, 2 Sam. 2.1–8, or *Iliad* 2.121–30), *except* when writing for some instructors in history, philosophy, religion, music, art, and theater, in which case you may need to use roman numerals (e.g., III, Act II, I Sam. ii.1–8, Hamlet I.ii.5–6).

Running Heads

Repeat your last name in the upper right corner of every page just in front of the page number (see the sample paper, page 158). APA style requires a short title with the page number.

Shortened Titles in the Text

Use abbreviated titles of books and articles mentioned often in the text after a first, full reference. For example, after its initial appearance, *Backgrounds to English as Language* should be shortened to *Backgrounds* in the text, notes, and in-text citations.

Spacing

As a general rule, double-space all typed material in your paper—the body, all indented quotations, and all reference entries. Footnotes, if used, should be single-spaced, but endnotes should be double-spaced (see page 173). APA style (see Chapter 11) requires double-spacing after all headings and separates text from indented quotes and from figures by double-spacing. Use one space after commas, semicolons, colons, and periods. Use one space after punctuation marks at the end of sentences. Do not use a space before or after a dash.

Titles within Titles

For a book title that includes another title indicated by quotation marks, retain the quotation marks.

<u>O. Henry's Irony in "The Gift of the Magi"</u>

For an article title that includes a book title, use italics or underlining for the book.

"<u>Great Expectations</u> as a Novel of Initiation"

For an article title that includes another title indicated by quotation marks, enclose the shorter title in single quotation marks.

"A Reading of O. Henry's 'The Gift of the Magi'"

For an underscored book title that incorporates another normally underscored title, do not underscore or italicize the shorter title nor place it within quotation marks.

<u>Interpretations of</u> Great Expectations

Underscoring (*Italicizing*)
Titles

Use italics or underscoring for the titles of the following types of works:

TYPE OF WORK	EXAMPLE
book	*A Quaker Book of Wisdom*
bulletin	*Production Memo 3*
drama	*Desire under the Elms*
film	*Treasure of the Sierra Madre*
journal	*Journal of Sociology*
magazine	*Newsweek*
newspaper	*Boston Globe*
novel	*Band of Angels*
poem (book length)	*Idylls of the King*
short novel	*Billy Budd*

In contrast, place quotation marks around titles of articles, essays, chapters, sections, short poems, stories, songs, lectures, sermons, reports, and individual episodes of television programs.

Do not underscore the titles of sacred writings (Genesis, Old Testament); series (The New American Nation Series); editions (Variorum Edition of W. B. Yeats); societies (Victorian Society); courses (Greek Mythology); divisions of a work (preface, appendix, canto 3, scene 2); or descriptive phrases (Nixon's farewell address or Reagan's White House years).

Word Division

Avoid dividing words at the end of a line, even if it makes one line of text extremely short.

Credits

Ch. 2 Figure 2.1 page 23
Entry "Victims of Crime" from *Bibliographic Index,* 2000. Copyright © 2000 by The H. W. Wilson Company. Reprinted by permission.

Ch. 2 Figure 2.2 page 25
Sample entry, "Brain Stimulation Implants" from *Reader's Guide to Periodical Literature,* May 2000. Copyright © 2000 by The H. W. Wilson Company. Reprinted by permission.

Ch. 2 Figure 2.3 page 28
From "Lawmaker: Home-Schoolers Shouldn't Have Tougher ACT Mark," by Duren Cheek, *The Tennessean,* October 23, 2003. Copyright © 2003 by *The Tennessean.* Reprinted by permission.

Ch. 5 page 60
From "The New Science of Alzheimer's" by J. Madeline Nash, *Time,* July 17, 2000. Copyright © 2000 by Time, Inc. Reprinted by permission.

Ch. 10 page 125
From "The Waste Land" in *Collected Poems 1901-1962* by T. S. Eliot. Reprinted by permission of the publisher, Faber and Faber Limited.

Ch. 10 page 126
Sophocles, "Oedipus Rex," *The Oedipus Cycle: An English Version* by Dudley Fitts and Robert Fitzgerald. New York: Harcourt, Brace, 1958, 1949.

Ch. 10 page 127
Elizabeth Barrett Browning, "The Cry of the Children," 1844.

Ch. 10 page 145
W. H. Auden, *Lectures on Shakespeare,* Ed. Arthur Kirsch. Princeton, NJ: Princeton University Press, 2000.

Ch. 14 Figure 14.1 page 190, Figure 14.2 page 191, and Figure 14.3 page 193
Keats photo ©Bettmann/CORBIS

Ch. 14 Figure 14.2 page 191
Grecian urn photo courtesy Scala/Art Resource, NY

Index

Bold page numbers indicate areas of primary discussion.

Citing an Internet Article
QUICK REFERENCE

APA Style (online journal article)

Dow, J. (2000). External and internal approaches to emotion: Commentary on Nesse on mood. *Psycoloquy, 10.* Retrieved October 15, 2003, from http://www.cogsci.soton.ac.uk/cgi/psyc/newpsy?3.01

MLA Style (online abstract)

Ladouceur, Robert, et al. "Strategies Used with Intrusive Thoughts: A Comparison of OCD Patients with Anxious and Community Controls." <u>Journal of Abnormal Psychology</u> 109 (2000). Abstract. 15 Oct. 2003 <http://www.apa.org/journals/abn/500ab.html>.

CMS Style (footnote)

13. B. A. Miller, N. J. Smyth, and P. J. Mudar, "Mothers' Alcohol and Other Drug Problems and Their Punitiveness toward Their Children," *Journal of Studies on Alcohol* 60 (1999), http://www.ncbi.nlm.hih.gov.htbin.

CSE Style (numbered bibliography entry)

4. Shane-McWhorter, L. Complementary and alternative medicine (CAM) in diabetes. Complementary andAlternative Medicine [serial online] 2002. Available from: http://www.childrenwithdiabetes.com/clinic/alternative. Accessed 2003 Aug 8.

The Essential Guide

Research Writing Across the Disciplines

Third Edition

James D. Lester
James D. Lester, Jr.

The Essential Guide: Research Writing Across the Disciplines is the ultimate brief research reference. Pocket-sized and inexpensive, this research guide is intended to supplement any course that requires research.

FEATURES

- Increased coverage of the library's electronic resources, including academic databases.

- Chapter 5 focuses on avoiding plagiarism and practicing academic integrity.

- Chapters 6 and 7 help students identify the best sources, evaluate them for relevance, authority, and accuracy and to create notes that paraphrase, quote, and summarize effectively.

- Complete and up-to-date coverage of four citation styles—MLA, APA, CSE, and *Chicago*. Also includes coverage of citing electronic sources in each of these styles.

Visit us at www.ablongman.com

PEARSON

Longman

ISBN 0-321-27639-6

90000

9 780321 276391